Roanoke Island

DAVID STICK

Roanoke Island
The Beginnings of
English America

Published for America's Four Hundredth

Anniversary Committee by the

University of North Carolina Press

Chapel Hill and London

© 1983 The University of North Carolina Press

Manufactured in the United States of America

First printing, November 1983
Second printing, February 1984
Third printing, June 1984

Library of Congress Cataloging in Publication Data

Stick, David, 1919–
  Roanoke Island, the beginnings of English America.

"Published for America's Four Hundredth Anniversary
Committee."
  Includes index.
  1. Roanoke Island (N.C.)—History. 2. America—
Discovery and exploration—English. I. North Carolina.
America's Four Hundredth Anniversary Committee. II. Title
F262.R4S74   1983   975.6'175   83-7014
ISBN 0-8078-1554-3
ISBN 0-8078-4110-2 (pbk.)

America's Four Hundredth Anniversary Committee and the
University of North Carolina Press gratefully acknowledge the
support of the Integon Foundation in the publication of this
book.

In memory of

Friend, scholar, and leader
in planning America's
Quadricentennial

Contents

Illustrations & Maps

ILLUSTRATIONS

MAPS

Preface

Twenty-two years before John Smith and the Jamestown settlers first sighted Chesapeake Bay and thirty-five years before *Mayflower* reached the coast of Massachusetts, the first English colony in America was established on Roanoke Island, in what is now North Carolina.

Explorers sent out by Sir Walter Raleigh landed on the North Carolina Outer Banks in 1584, taking possession in the name of Queen Elizabeth. Between then and 1587 there was a steady stream of shipping between England and Raleigh's Roanoke Island settlement, with such renowned Elizabethans as Sir Francis Drake and Sir Richard Grenville taking part. The vast area covered by Raleigh's patent, comprising much of what is now the United States, was named "Virginia" in honor of the Virgin Queen. A force under Ralph Lane spent a year there, exploring as far north as Chesapeake Bay, inspecting most of the villages in the Albemarle Sound area, and traveling far up the Chowan and Roanoke rivers.

Permanency seemed assured in 1587 when a colony of men, women, and children arrived at Roanoke Island. That summer the Indian Manteo was baptized—the first Protestant baptism in the New World. A baby girl, Virginia Dare, was born—the first child born of English parents in America. But for the next three years all efforts to provide relief for the settlement were thwarted by war with Spain and by King Philip's mighty Spanish Armada.

When an expedition finally arrived in 1590, the settlers had disappeared, to be known thereafter as Sir Walter Raleigh's "lost colony."

As the four hundredth anniversary of Raleigh's settlements and the lost colony approaches, it is important to focus attention on Roanoke Island and the beginnings of English America. Much has already been written about these colonization efforts, but the bulk of it has been either too scholarly to hold the attention of the lay reader, or fictionalized. This book has been written at the request of America's Four Hundredth Anniversary Committee to fill a void between those scholarly and fictionalized works. The specific charge to the author was to produce a concise, accurate, "popularly written" book for the average reader. Certainly, after much cutting and rewriting, it is concise; and every effort has been made to ensure its accuracy. It remains for the individual reader to judge the popularity of the style.

William S. Powell, publications chairman of the Four Hundredth Anniversary Committee and long-time friend and fellow historian, has provided guidance and encouragement from the outset, and has carefully read and edited the manuscript in two different stages. John D. Neville, Philip W. Evans, and the late Herbert R. Paschal, Jr., provided valuable input as the book took shape. Wynne C. Dough, associate and adviser, has corrected spelling and punctuation, double-checked sources, and read proofs, all with no outward sign of complaint. David Perry has edited the book for the University of North Carolina Press and has seen it through the various phases of the publication process.

It is impossible for anyone writing about Raleigh and his colonies to express adequate appreciation to David B. Quinn, and his wife and research associate, Alison M. Quinn, for bringing together the source material. To a large degree their efforts have made it possible for the rest of us to understand what went on here and in England four hundred years ago. And without the writings of Arthur Barlowe, Ralph Lane, and Thomas Hariot—and the accounts and drawings of John White—so ably published four centuries ago by Theodor de Bry and Richard Hakluyt, we would have little accurate information from which to draw for this story of true adventure.

From the outset it was the intent of America's Four Hundredth Anniversary Committee, in this day of escalating publication costs, to make this book available in both hardbound and paperback editions at a reasonable price. A generous publishing subvention by the Integon Foundation, Inc., has made this possible.

David Stick
Kitty Hawk
February, 1983

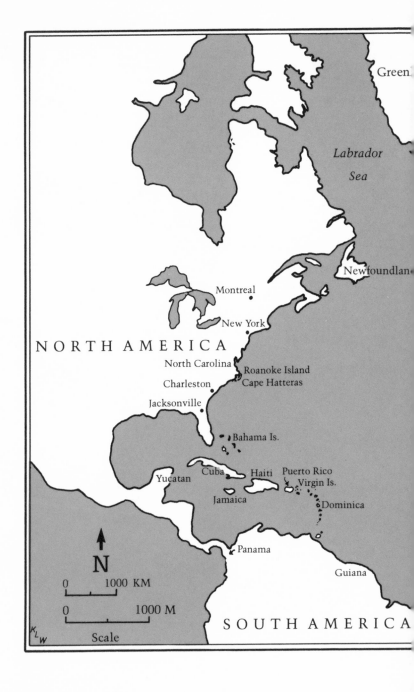

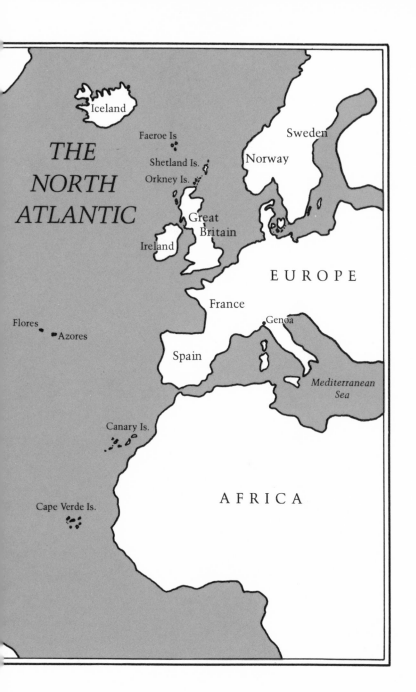

THE
NORTH
ATLANTIC

Iceland

Faeroe Is

Shetland Is.

Orkney Is.

Sweden

Norway

Great
Britain

Ireland

EUROPE

Flores

Azores

France

Genoa

Spain

Mediterranean
Sea

Canary Is.

AFRICA

Cape Verde Is.

Introduction

   Anyone making a study of the early European efforts to colonize America must inevitably ask the question: Why were the English so late getting into the act?

As every school child knows—or should know—the first voyage of discovery by Columbus was in the year 1492. Yet it was nearly a century later, in the 1580s, when men, women, and children sent out by Sir Walter Raleigh established the first English colonies in America—on Roanoke Island, in an area the Elizabethans called Virginia, now the state of North Carolina.

In order to understand the reasons for this late start by the English it is necessary to review the history of European discovery and settlement in America, and to gain an understanding of the extent of man's knowledge—or lack of knowledge—of world geography in the centuries preceding permanent settlement in this hemisphere.

Following his "discovery" of America, Columbus made three more voyages across the Atlantic, exploring the islands of the Caribbean and touching on the coasts of both Central America and South America. Yet he had no understanding of where he had been, let alone any awareness of the magnitude of his discoveries.

In fact, Columbus died in the firm belief that he had reached the Indies, a name applied in the fifteenth century to a vast area that included China, Japan, and the islands of Indonesia. He was certain when he arrived in the Caribbean that he was really just off the coast of Cathay, or China, and that Cuba was actually the legendary Cipango, or Japan.

If voices were raised back in Europe suggesting that Columbus was in error, and that in fact he had discovered a previously unknown hemisphere midway between Europe and Asia, they were quickly stilled. The returning hero had reached the Indies. The natives he encountered in that far-off land were thus Indians. And to this day the islands he really discovered in the Caribbean are known as the West Indies, not to be confused with those on the other side of the world he thought he had reached, the East Indies.

The Columbus mistake—roughly equivalent to our astronauts landing on a previously unknown planet instead of the moon and not knowing the difference—is understandable when one considers the limited knowledge of world geography five hundred years ago. Nearly two thousand years earlier some scientists and philosophers had concluded that the earth was round, largely as a result of data developed by Aristotle and Eratosthenes. But information was lacking on the size of the earth, on the portions of the surface covered by land or by water, and on the shape and extent of the land masses.

The European ancients were aware that temperatures became colder as one traveled to the north, and warmer to the south, but since their knowledge was limited to their own immediate areas, they could only speculate on what lay beyond.

For centuries it was believed that travelers heading south would reach a zone in which temperatures were too hot to sustain life in any form, and that any mariner so foolhardy as to approach this "burning zone" below the Equator would perish. Thus few explorers sailing south along the west coast of Africa dared to venture more than a few hundred miles from the Mediterranean, though folklore and some evidence has been uncovered to fortify the claim—a very weak claim—that Phoenicians sailed around the southern tip of Africa before the Christian era began.

As for the vast Atlantic Ocean stretching westward from Europe, there was speculation that it ended in an impenetrable quagmire or in a monstrous, steaming whirlpool, or even that it merged with and became part of the sky. Many referred to it as the "Sea of Darkness," and some who had ventured beyond the sight of land and viewed that awesome phenomenon in which the waters on the far horizon seem to slope downward with the curvature of the earth were convinced that once they started sailing down that slope, it would be impossible to sail back up again.

Much more was known of the area to the north. It is generally believed by modern historians that Irish monks seeking areas sufficiently isolated to preclude any possibility of their having contact with women, sailed north and west as far as Iceland and established monasteries there as early as the fifth or sixth centuries A.D. One of the monks, St. Brendan of Clonfert, is recorded as having sailed across part or all of the Atlantic in search of the "Promised Land of the Saints." It is also entirely possible that mariners venturing too far into the Atlantic may have encountered storms so severe as to have blown their frail craft across the broad expanses of the sea to fetch up on the coast of North America or South America, though nothing more than vague hints of such occurrences remain.

Most information on early exploration comes down to us through the words of ancient poets and philosophers, transmitted for the most part by word of mouth for centuries before finally being put down in writing. Any such information must therefore be viewed with skepticism, if not outright disbelief, until archaeological discovery or the uncovering of additional documentation provides further corroboration. Even now such studies are being undertaken to investigate stories of early crossings of the Pacific by Chinese seamen. Other researchers are trying to discern the meaning of inscriptions found on the remains of ancient structures in New England said to be of Celtic origin dating back as much as three thousand years.

Of all the claims of early exploration in this hemisphere the ones given the most credence by historians are the accounts of the Norsemen, who established a new homeland in Iceland more than a thousand years ago, for theirs are the earliest detailed written records of European exploration on the western side of the Atlantic. These accounts of the Norse settlements in Iceland, and later in Greenland—mostly family records of the type sought by modern genealogists—are further substantiated by the discovery of the ruins of many of their structures, including seventeen at a single site in Greenland. These records were not written down until at least two centuries after the events took place, and thus are flawed if one accepts them as more than a general outline. But they tell a fascinating story and provide a beginning point for any chronology of European settlement in America.

For those concerned with exact dates, this bold Icelandic adventure can be traced—according to the Norse records—to the year 872, when King Harold Fairhair, after twelve years of war, was victorious over a confederation of independent princes, known as jarls, and their Viking followers. These proud Vikings—the name means "men of the fjords" or "men of the bays"—were, by desire as much as by training, shipbuilders, mariners, and explorers alike. To them "the sea was not a barrier, but a highway," and the prospect of subordination to their conqueror, King Harold, was intolerable.

Leaving their native Norway to seek new lands to call their own, they fanned out over the waterways of the known world, some traveling in their dragon-prowed vessels to the Mediterranean, others to Scotland and Ireland, and still others to those isolated chains of small islands in the Atlantic off the Norwegian coast: the Orkneys, the Shetlands, and the Faeroes. Some of the more adventuresome sailed still farther west, arriving finally in Iceland and finding it truly the land of promise they had been seeking.

The soil and climatic conditions in Iceland made possible heavy crops of hay, so that the Vikings' sheep and cattle flourished. A lively trade was established with Norway, Denmark, and the British Isles. Meal and malt were imported in exchange for fish, oil, butter, skins, and wool. In the words of nineteenth-century historian John Fiske, "Political freedom was unimpaired, justice was (for the Middle Ages) fairly well administered, naval superiority kept all foes at a distance; and under such conditions the growth of the new community in wealth and culture was surprisingly rapid."

Though the population of Iceland grew quickly, it was more than a hundred years after the arrival of those original Viking colonists before a serious effort was made to explore the uncharted area to the west. Finally, in 983, a settler in western-most Iceland named Eric Thorvaldson, but better known as Eric the Red, was outlawed for killing a man in a brawl. With a few adventurous followers he set out on his own voyage of discovery, seeking a new homeland much as his Viking ancestors had done.

Eric had heard stories, passed down by the elders, of an early Icelandic settler named Gunnbjorn who had spent a winter on the coast of a large island to the west, his vessel locked in ice. It was not long before Eric reached Gunnbjorn's island, and in three years of exploring its coastline he learned that it was a huge land mass, many times the size of Iceland, but largely covered with ice and glaciers. On its southern tip, however, he found an ideal location for his settlement, a deep fjord, or bay, almost hidden "by miles upon miles of craggy and ice-covered headlands."

The small band set about building houses, ensuring permanency by using native sandstone blocks held in place with a mortar made of clay and gravel. Located on a large grassy plain overlooking the fjord, the new community was a veritable oasis of green in those bleak surroundings, so Eric called the settlement Greenland, a name later erroneously applied to all of that vast white land of glaciers and snow-capped peaks.

Eric was the father of at least one daughter, Freydis, and three sons, Thorvald, Thorstein, and Leif. All four were involved in American discovery, but it is his son Leif—whose name has come down to us as Leif Eriksson rather than as "Leif, Eric's son" or "Eric's son, Leif"—who is generally acknowledged to have established the first European settlement on North American soil.

On a visit to Norway, in the course of which he was baptized as a Christian, Leif heard intriguing stories of the exploits several years earlier of a Norwegian mariner and explorer named Bjarni Herjolfsson. According to these accounts Bjarni had sailed from Norway in the year 985, bound for Iceland for no better reason than to join his father for Christmas, but on arrival there he learned that his father was with Eric the Red in Greenland. It was typical of the fearless and adventuresome Norsemen that Bjarni decided to sail off into the vast unknown to the west of Iceland in the hope of locating his father. The members of his crew seemed to share this spirit of adventure, for it is recorded in the *Saga of the Greenlanders* that even after Bjarni admitted to his men that "this voyage of ours will be considered foolhardy, for not one of us has ever sailed the Greenland Sea," none refused to embark with him.

Soon after sailing beyond sight of the Icelandic coast, Bjarni's vessel was becalmed, then engulfed by a dense blanket of fog. When the winds finally picked up, they came with a vengeance, constantly buffeting the small craft while driving it ever southward, and for many days they were unable to mark their course.

When at last the storm subsided and the skies brightened enough for Bjarni to take bearings, he set a course he hoped would lead to Greenland. The second day land was sighted, and though his men urged him to make a landing, Bjarni refused to do so, explaining that this could not possibly be Greenland. There is little question that at that moment Bjarni and his crew had discovered the mainland of North America.

Three more times on their voyage northward the men of Norway sighted land, and each time Bjarni refused to go ashore, certain they had not reached Greenland, for he had heard that there were huge glaciers in Greenland, whereas the land they had sighted was covered with hills and forests. Ten days after starting their voyage northward, and aided most of the time by fresh southerly winds, they finally sighted glacier-covered land. It was, in fact, Greenland. Even more amazing, they shortly made contact with Bjarni's father, though it is not recorded whether they had reached him in time for the Christmas celebration.

Back in Norway there was considerable talk about Bjarni's exploits and disappointment that he had not made at least one landing on the forested hillsides he and his men described. Not until Leif Eriksson heard the stories some fifteen years later, however, was anyone sufficiently interested to consider investigating further. Leif made personal contact with Bjarni, learned firsthand of the details of the venture, then arranged to purchase Bjarni's ship for an expedition of his own.

Leif enlisted a thirty-five-man crew, returned to Greenland, and set out to retrace Bjarni's voyage—in reverse. The first land Leif sighted was bare and covered with huge flat rocks. Landing on this barren coast, Leif gave it a name, Helluland (Slabland), and declared, though it seemed worthless, that he and his men had "done better than Bjarni where this country is concerned—we at least have set foot on it."

Two days later they landed again, this time finding the terrain more hospitable and pleasant, with the flat wooded land sloping gently toward sandy beaches at the edge of the sea. "This country shall be named after its natural resources," Leif declared. "It shall be called *Markland* [Woodland]."

Again they put out to sea, and after sailing before a northeast wind for two more days they sighted land. Waiting until early morning to go ashore, they found dew on the grass and went through a ritual of rubbing their hands in the dew then moistening their lips, declaring it to be "the sweetest thing they had ever tasted." Returning to their ship, they explored the area, finding a protected harbor in which they were soon stranded, high and dry, as the tide receded. So great was their excitement at finding this ideal spot for a settlement that these men of Greenland could not wait for the rising tide, but waded ashore, soon discovering a river flowing into the harbor and a short distance inland a lagoonlike lake, deep yet tranquil. Returning to the ship, they sailed up the river with the tide and anchored in the lake. They had arrived at their new home.

Selecting a site near the shore of the lake, they built temporary shelters, then set about constructing more permanent structures. The exact location of this first known European settlement on the North American mainland, established by Leif Eriksson in the year 1000, has been the subject of speculation and disagreement for centuries. For a while there was serious contention that it was on the coast of Massachusetts, but most historians now seem to feel that it was much more to the north, possibly on the coast of Labrador.

When the buildings were completed, Leif divided his men into two groups and sent them off on foot exploring the surrounding area, the two parties making their forays on alternate days so that half of the company would always be at the home base. On one of these overland expeditions they came upon a great profusion of grapevines, prompting Leif to name the country Vinland. They then set about selecting and cutting down trees, and with a cargo of timber and vines they left beautiful Vinland and set sail on a northward course, reaching home after an uneventful voyage.

There is no indication that Leif Eriksson ever returned to Vinland, but his account of the verdant land to the south enthralled other members of his family, and over the next ten years both of his brothers and his sister left Greenland on expeditions to Vinland. His brother Thorvald reached the North American mainland in 1002 and for two years explored the coast in the summer months, using Leif's houses as a winter base. Another brother, Thorstein, died at sea soon after leaving Greenland on a voyage to Vinland in 1005. But two years later his widow, having remarried, embarked with her new husband, Thorfinn Karlsefni, on yet another expedition and spent three or four years on the North American continent before giving up the attempt at colonization.

The final effort to settle Leif's Vinland came in 1011. Eric's daughter Freydis and her husband, Thorvard, led the expedition, followed by a second vessel under the command of brothers named Helgi and Finnbogi. They were successful in reaching Vinland, but disagreement over which crew should occupy Leif's original buildings led to open hostility, culminating in the murder of Helgi, Finnbogi, and all of their followers. On this gruesome note all Norse attempts to establish a permanent colony on the North American mainland ended.

There was a lapse of nearly five hundred years after the Norse attempts at colonization in Vinland before Christopher Columbus "discovered" America. If one were to try to put this in a modern perspective, it would be as though the Europeans had made no effort for five hundred years to follow up on the voyages of exploration made by Columbus, and were just now deciding to check them out.

A partial explanation for the five centuries of inactivity is that the Greenlanders themselves seem not to have considered the discoveries of enough importance to warrant further exploration, and memories and stories of the exploits of Leif Eriksson and his brothers and sister were no doubt dimmed with the passing of each succeeding generation. The eventual abandonment of the Norse settlements in Greenland would indicate, also, that the descendants of the Vikings had enough problems at home without looking for others beyond the horizon. Finally, the glorious era of the intrepid Viking explorers had passed, and with the passing went their compelling motivation to sail the uncharted seas in bold search of new homelands and adventure.

The motivation that drove Christopher Columbus was of a different sort. His was not the quest for a new land to escape oppression at home. Nor was he a Bjarni Herjolfsson, almost casually searching the unknown waters of the western world in order to rejoin his father for Christmas— and somehow managing to find him in the bleak and foreboding vastness of Greenland.

Rather, Columbus appeared to be driven by an all-consuming desire, an obsession really, to accomplish a specific objective, one so deeply embedded in his being that no amount of failure or frustration could stay him from the quest. For Columbus was convinced that he could sail west from Europe on the "Sea of Darkness" and reach the Indies, thus opening a direct trade route by sea to the fabled riches of China, Japan, and Indonesia.

Silk, spices, and other exotic products of the Far East had begun trickling into the Mediterranean area many centuries earlier, long before any recorded visit of a European to Asia, or of an Asian to Europe. No doubt these commodities had been passed along in a totally unplanned and haphazard manner from one merchant to another, moving by caravan and by backpack and changing hands at every trading center along the route until at last a roll of Chinese silk, for example, might have finally reached Egypt or Greece.

The discoveries of Marco Polo in the late thirteenth

century figured prominently in the opening of direct overland trade routes with Asia. Polo spent seventeen years in China, and his written account, the *Travels of Marco Polo*, captivated Europeans—merchants, explorers, and potentates alike. But such an overland venture covered thousands of miles and involved passing through innumerable countries, fiefdoms, and tribal territories. Transporting cargo by camel, by horse, by boat, and even on foot was dangerous, uncertain, time consuming, and, above all else, expensive. Inevitably, men would begin to think of alternatives.

By the time of the birth of Columbus in Genoa (probably in 1451, although the exact date is uncertain) a sufficient number of Europeans had been to China to comprehend that the Asian continent did not extend to infinity and that it was not bordered on the east by an impenetrable swamp, as had been supposed. Instead, the eastern shore of China was bounded by an open sea, "and half a dozen Europeans in Chinese ships had now actually made the voyage between the coast of China and the Persian Gulf," thus putting them within hundreds, rather than thousands, of miles of the Mediterranean.

In the search for a connecting link explorers sailed south along the west coast of Africa with the hope that before entering the burning zone the shoreline would trend eastward, and join the Persian Gulf waters. But when these explorers, mostly Portuguese, found no such connection after sailing nearly four thousand miles along the African coast, they ceased the effort and concentrated on extracting what treasures they could from the newly discovered African territories, with emphasis at first on yellow gold, then on black slaves.

Meanwhile, other bold explorers had found light in the Sea of Darkness, rediscovering and colonizing the Madeira, Canary, and Cape Verde islands off the African coast and sailing across nearly a thousand miles of open sea to the Azores.

Columbus is recorded as having first gone to sea at the

age of fourteen, and by the time his great dream took shape, he was a mariner of extensive experience, having sailed as far south as the Gold Coast and as far west as Iceland. On one voyage he was shipwrecked off the coast of Portugal and managed to swim ashore, and for years thereafter he made Portugal his base of operations. The efforts of this Italian-born adventurer to seek support for his grand venture in Portugal were encumbered by the conditions he placed on his service. A beggar he may have been, but he was begging for a full-course meal, not just a cup of coffee. He demanded not only the best of ships, fully equipped, but complete control over the expedition, plus a large share of any profits that might result, and even a title to satisfy his vanity. This seemed too much for the king of Portugal, and in time Columbus sought support in Spain.

Columbus arrived in Spain in 1484. Within two years he had made a sufficient impression on people of importance, including King Ferdinand and Queen Isabella, to be listed as being in their service and receiving financial support from the crown. For years the merits of his plan were debated in and out of court, but the turning point did not come until he acquired a partner in the person of Martín Alonso Pinzón, a respected pilot and shipowner residing in the Spanish seaport of Palos. Concern that Columbus might have received French or English backing also figured in the decision of Ferdinand and Isabella to accede to Columbus's extraordinary demands: He was to be knighted and made grand admiral and viceroy of the areas he discovered and was to receive 10 percent of all merchandise he acquired, with special emphasis on pearls, precious stones, gold, silver, and spices.

Columbus and Pinzón departed from Palos half an hour before sunrise on the morning of August 3, 1492. Their fleet consisted of three small but fully equipped vessels, the *Pinta*, the *Niña*, and the *Santa María*. Approximately two-thirds of the cost of the expedition had been provided by Ferdinand and Isabella, and modern historians seem convinced that Ferdinand was as enthusiastic a backer as was his queen, thus debunking the folktale that Isabella had pawned her jewels to provide the financing. The remaining one-third was Columbus's share, though the necessary funds had been lent or advanced to him by Pinzón.

From the time the ships departed the quay at Palos, Columbus had no doubt about where he was going and what he would find. He was certain that Japan was on the other side of the Atlantic approximately twenty-five hundred miles due west of the Canary Islands, so he headed for the Canaries, laid over there a little more than a week to take on fresh water and provisions, and finally on September 6 set sail again on a direct westerly course to the Indies. Had he remained on that heading, Columbus and Pinzón would have landed on the northern coast of Florida, but after traveling the estimated twenty-five hundred miles without sight of land Columbus assumed that the three vessels were passing north of Japan, so he altered his course in a more southerly direction.

There had already been considerable dissatisfaction among the crewmen, some of whom were convinced they would never set foot on land again, let alone return to Spain in safety. Anticipating the possibility of just such a development, Columbus had turned to a subterfuge soon after leaving the Canary Islands to prevent his men from knowing the true distance they had traveled. It was a neat bit of deception in which he kept two different sets of records, one for himself, and the other for the crew. A typical entry in the log, for September 10, showed they had covered 144 miles in the twenty-four-hour period, whereas Columbus actually figured the distance—and so entered it in his private journal—as 180 miles. The next day the official figure was listed as 108 miles, when in fact he reckoned the distance traveled to have been 120. By this devious method he almost certainly averted mutiny.

With the change in course the three tiny vessels were

headed for the Bahama Islands rather than Florida, and on October 7 the lookout on the *Niña* thought he spotted land, though it turned out to be an illusion. Birds were seen, however, and floating reeds, and all that night they heard birds in flight until, at dawn, they found themselves approaching a small island.

That day Columbus and his lieutenants went ashore for the first time in their newly discovered land, taking possession in the name of Ferdinand and Isabella and naming the island San Salvador (now Guanahaní, or Watling Island). For the next two weeks they wandered among the islands, landing frequently, raising crosses, and bestowing Spanish names on the islands and cays. Columbus was convinced more than ever that these were some of "the islands which are set down on the maps at the end of the Orient."

Thus, at last, was America properly discovered—a previously unknown hemisphere and two new continents, even if no one was aware of it.

From the time of these initial discoveries in 1492 until 1506 Columbus made four voyages to America and spent nearly half of that fourteen-year period in the West Indies. His career is a paradox of triumph and failure, of exultation and despair. He returned from one voyage of discovery a hero in whose presence his reigning king and queen rose from their thrones in tribute; from another in chains; and from yet another, his last one, a man so broken in mind and spirit that he had to be conveyed from his vessel on a stretcher.

Year after year, persisting in his belief that he had reached Asia, he sailed, sometimes almost aimlessly, throughout the Caribbean. He touched once on the mainland of South America, which he was certain was just another little island, and on Cuba, so convinced that the latter was Japan that he forced the members of his crew to sign an affidavit to that effect, whether they believed it or not. As viceroy and admiral of the Indies, he installed two of his brothers in positions of power, took his thirteen-year-old son on one of his voyages, massacred native Indians, took others as slaves, and hanged subordinates who questioned his authority.

By the time of his last voyage, though, it had become almost commonplace for European mariners to sail through the once dreaded Sea of Darkness, and several thousand European men had made the passage. In the process, innumerable islands throughout the Caribbean had been discovered and named, permanent settlements had been established on several of the larger islands, and exploring expeditions had proceeded as far north as Labrador and as far south as the coast of Brazil.

Spain continued to solidify its dominance in America, and in less than half a century its emissaries had explored, conquered, and colonized a whole new world. The names of most of those responsible for expanding the Spanish claim are well known: Ponce de León, Magellan, Elcano, Ayllón, de Soto, Balboa, Cortés, Pizarro.

The portrayal of Ponce de León as a sort of maritime Don Quixote, endlessly searching the bays and cays of the Caribbean for the mythical Fountain of Youth, is fiction; but as is so often the case, it is based on fact. After leading the first extensive explorations of Puerto Rico and establishing that island's first settlement, he embarked on a voyage of discovery with two quite different objectives in mind: to locate and claim new lands for Spain, and to search out the Fountain of Youth.

In 1513, leaving the island of Bimini, in the Bahamas, Ponce de León landed at Easter time (*Pascua Florida* in Spanish) on what he thought was yet another of the multitude of islands in that area. Since no one was aware that the Florida he had discovered and named was actually a peninsula occupying the extreme southeastern corner of North America, Ponce de León's exploits hardly caused a murmur in either the Spanish West Indies or the Spanish homeland. In 1521, on a follow-up expedition along the west coast of Florida, his small force was attacked by Indians, and Ponce de León was wounded. He lived long enough to return to Havana, and there this relatively peaceful New World pioneer died.

The exploits of Ferdinand Magellan and Sebastián d'Elcano are among the most remarkable of the period. Magellan, a native of Portugal, headed an expedition which departed Spain in 1519 in search of new routes to Asia. Elcano was master of one of Magellan's ships. Crossing the Atlantic to South America, they sailed down the coast, rounded Cape Horn, and entered the "Sea of the South," which Magellan named the Pacific Ocean because its waters were so calm at the time of their crossing. When Magellan was killed in a fight with natives on an island in the Philippines in 1521, Elcano continued the voyage, and returned finally to Spain in a single ship with just 17 surviving crewmen of the 270 who had set sail in Magellan's five-vessel fleet nearly three years earlier. Thus Sebastián d'Elcano, rather than Ferdinand Magellan, was the first circumnavigator of the globe.

Meanwhile, in the West Indies plans were being made to launch the first attempt at colonizing the mainland of North America with citizens of Spain. The main force behind the movement was Lucas Vázquez de Ayllón, a man of wealth and influence, whose emissaries had already explored the Carolina coast, returning in triumph with a number of Indian slaves. Ayllón's plans were for discovery and settlement, not slave hunting, and he ordered all of the Indians returned—all, that is, except one, whom he had baptized and named Francisco of Chicora.

As he sought and finally secured royal support for settling the new lands, Ayllón was no doubt aided by Francisco, whose lurid stories of life on the continent helped to arouse interest in the venture.

While waiting for the response from Spain, Ayllón was involved in yet another exploring expedition, this one with Pedro de Quexos, who discovered a river, thought to be the Cape Fear, which he named the River Jordan.

In 1526, Ayllón was ready for his colonizing effort. He acquired three large ships, assembled a company of some six hundred people, including women, children, and Negro slaves, and, after deciding against trying to establish a colony in the area of the River Jordan, finally found the site he wanted near Winyah Bay in what is now South Carolina. Ayllón named the settlement San Miguel de Guadalupe, and his colonists set about building houses and clearing land, which they found to be flat with considerable areas of marsh. The early death of Ayllón, from a fever, marked the beginning of the end for this first serious colonization effort in what is now the United States. Soon thereafter the slaves rebelled, local Indians attacked, and the remaining settlers abandoned San Miguel de Guadalupe. Even in retreat, however, bad luck continued, for the weather turned so bitter cold that seven men were reported to have frozen to death before they reached the warmer climate to the south.

The discovery of Florida by Ponce de León and the efforts to establish a colony by Ayllón provided only enticing tidbits of information about the vast continent to the north and west of the Caribbean. It was left to Hernando de Soto, a man of wealth and standing, to lead a truly amazing expedition deep into the mainland of the American continent. Landing on the west coast of Florida in 1539 with an impressive force consisting of one thousand men and 350 horses, he spent the winter near Tallahassee, explored the Gulf coast, then turned north. Alternately making treaties with friendly Indians and engaging in battle with those who resisted its advance, the de Soto expedition is thought to have traveled as far north as western Tennessee before dipping back into Mississippi, Arkansas, and possibly even Oklahoma, always seeking but never finding reputed Indian cities of great wealth. On the trip back down the Mississippi toward the Gulf, de Soto died in Louisiana, and his body was ceremoniously offered up to the great river to prevent his remains from falling into the hands of the Indians.

By the time of the de Soto explorations those other Spanish adventurers known as conquistadors—most notably Vasco Núñez de Balboa, Hernán Cortés, and Francisco Pizarro—had conquered and looted much of Central America and South America, in the process effectively destroying the great Aztec and Inca civilizations in Mexico and Peru.

These Spanish activities, from Columbus to de Soto, had been observed with keen interest by England, Portugal, and France, the principal challengers to Spain's maritime dominance. Initially the English, Portuguese, and French leaders shared the belief that Columbus had in truth opened a direct route to Asia, and they envisioned a vast and as-yet-unexplored area of great potential wealth, extending from the islands of Indonesia along the entire coast of China to Japan. Convinced that there was thus no reason to challenge Spanish claims to what they considered only a small corner of Asia, they shied away from the West Indies in their early explorations.

England had been the first to react to the Columbus discoveries, sending out an expedition in 1496 under the command of an Italian mariner, John Cabot, a native of Genoa, the same city in which Columbus was born. Cabot was forced back by a combination of bad weather, a mutinous crew, and shortages of food, but on his return to England he began making plans for another attempt to reach China. His second voyage, in a single small vessel with eighteen men, lasted only three months, but he planted the first English flag on the North American mainland, in what is now Canada, thus establishing in 1497 an English claim to territory in the Western Hemisphere. The results of a third and much more ambitious expedition by Cabot the following year are shrouded in mystery, and it is doubtful that he ever again reached America, though his son, Sebastian, subsequently was engaged in a fruitless effort to locate a northern passage to Asia.

Portugal, whose sailors and navigators had long been considered among the world's best, took up where Cabot and England had left off, sending out expeditions in 1500, 1501, and 1502 under the command of two highly placed and experienced mariners, the brothers Gaspar and Miguel Corte-Real, who explored the northern coast of America in the vicinity of Labrador and the Bay of Fundy.

At about the same time Portugal backed another expedition, this one south of the Equator, under Amerigo Vespucci. Born in Italy and trained as a merchant, Vespucci was sent to Spain in 1491 at age thirty-seven as an agent for an Italian firm engaged in the business of outfitting ships. He was involved in preparing a vessel for the second voyage of Columbus and others for the third voyage, then abandoned his business career and decided to become an active participant in the momentous events transpiring across the Atlantic. He participated in one Spanish expedition, and perhaps two, to American waters but became frustrated in his efforts to secure backing for a Spanish voyage of his own and decided to seek support in Portugal. Whether by luck or by design, Vespucci picked the right country, and at just the right time, for the Portuguese, smarting over their failure to back the highly successful undertakings of Columbus, were embarking on their own program of discovery and had already dispatched the Corte-Real brothers on their northern voyage.

Vespucci set sail in May, 1501, and explored the South American coast at least as far as Brazil. In the process he became convinced that the lands he visited were not Asia, China, and Indonesia, as previously supposed, but were, in fact, a newly discovered continent. It was this revelation by Amerigo Vespucci, rather than any significance that might be attached to his discoveries of new territories, that resulted in his name being given initially to the southern part of the new hemisphere, and later to North America as well.

But that was it! Thus ended for more than half a century

English and Portuguese attempts to explore the New World. The question, of course, is why both of these established nations gave up so easily after the relatively feeble efforts of the Cabots, the Corte-Real brothers, and Vespucci. The answer appears both obvious and complex.

At the outset there was the matter of maritime power. Portugal, the land of seafarers, was a leader in voyages of exploration, but not in naval might. England, the island kingdom, was at that time a second-rate naval force, and had too many internal problems to get deeply involved in the New World. Spain was already emerging as the western world's dominant sea power, and its success in extracting seemingly endless wealth from America enabled it to buy almost anything it needed in order to gain and maintain its maritime superiority. Thus, the longer its would-be challengers backed off from a direct confrontation, the more secure was Spain's claim to its new dominions.

There was yet another reason why England and Portugal did not follow up the discoveries of Cabot and the Corte-Reals and establish their own colonies in the land they had begun to explore to the north, far from the Spanish areas of control in the West Indies and southern America. Winters in the maritime provinces of Canada, in Labrador for instance, or even Newfoundland or Nova Scotia, are harsh. The difficulties to be encountered there in trying to secure food and shelter, even in sustaining life, are considerably greater than in the balmy climate of the tropical West Indies. Moreover, gold and gems and bountiful treasure were easily taken from the Aztecs and Caribs and Incas, while Canada seemed to yield only codfish. No wonder the English and Portuguese gave up so easily.

The French, of course, were equally aware of Spain's newfound wealth and interested in trying to get their piece of the American action, but France was in no better position to launch a direct challenge to Spain than were the other European nations.

The French waited for more than two decades after the

voyages of the Corte-Real brothers before sending out their own exploring party, ostensibly to search for a passage through the North American continent to China. As had Spain with Columbus, England with Cabot, and Portugal with Vespucci, the king of France turned to Italy for an experienced mariner and navigator to undertake the French explorations across the Atlantic. In 1524, Giovanni da Verrazano, a native of Florence, in a single vessel with a crew of some fifty men, sailed due west from the northern coast of Africa, deliberately staying far above the route to the established Spanish bases.

Verrazano's initial landfall in America is thought to have been in the vicinity of Cape Fear. After a cursory examination of the adjacent coastline he sailed north along the Outer Banks of North Carolina, which he described as "an isthmus a mile in width and about 200 long." Verrazano assumed that Pamlico Sound, the broad inland body of water back of the Outer Banks islands, was an extension of the Pacific Ocean, a monumental error in judgment which resulted in this essentially landlocked sound being shown on maps for more than a century as "Verrazano's Sea." Proceeding still farther north he somehow missed the entrance to Chesapeake Bay, but explored the Hudson River and continued along the coast as far as Newfoundland. On a subsequent voyage, this one to the coast of South America, Verrazano is reported to have been captured, killed, and eaten by natives.

The North American discoveries of Verrazano served to whet the French appetite, and in 1534 a French mariner named Jacques Cartier crossed the North Atlantic and explored the Gulf of St. Lawrence. Returning for a second voyage, Cartier was icebound in the St. Lawrence River and spent a miserably cold winter holed up near Montreal. For the next five years France was occupied with more pressing business, most notably war with Spain, and it was not until 1541 that further plans could be made for colonization in America. This time a nobleman, Jean-

François de la Rocque de Roberval, was given command of the expedition, with Cartier serving under him. Disagreement between the two principals was as much a hindrance as the inhospitable weather for these would-be colonists, and Roberval gave up after Frenchmen had spent two more winters in Canada.

The French ardor for New World settlement was cooled considerably by the failure of the Cartier and Roberval colonization efforts on the St. Lawrence, and two more decades passed before they made another attempt to establish an outpost on the North American continent. But this one was quite different from those earlier, cautious efforts to carve off a little slice of the frozen American northland in an area so far removed from the West Indies as to pose no possible threat to Spanish control. Instead, this constituted the first direct and carefully calculated move to challenge Spain's American empire, for the locale chosen was Florida itself.

The project began in 1562 with an exploratory voyage under the command of Jean Ribaut, who established an outpost near Port Royal on the coast of South Carolina which he called Charlesfort. Ribaut left a detachment of thirty men to defend the French base, but when he failed to return at the appointed time from a voyage back to France for supplies and reinforcements, the men at Charlesfort built a small pinnace and headed out across the open sea toward home, finally making it after being picked up by a friendly English vessel.

Meanwhile careful preparations were being made for the establishment of a permanent and much larger settlement, this one even closer to Spain's colonial heartland. René de Laudonnière was given command of the force that departed France in early 1564 with three hundred men and three ships—including a sizable man-of-war—at his disposal. In the vicinity of the St. Johns River, near the modern city of Jacksonville, Florida, Laudonnière established his new French base, naming it Fort Caroline. Ribaut followed, in command of a large fleet with colonists, including women and children, on board, thus providing an aura of domesticity and permanency to the colony.

Soon after Ribaut's arrival, however, news came of the approach of a formidable fleet of Spanish warships, which had been assembled by Pedro Menéndez de Avilés for the specific purpose of annihilating the French intruders. Ribaut attempted to save his smaller vessels by weighing anchor and putting out to sea, but the strategy failed. Ribaut's vessels grounded or were wrecked before clearing the coast, enabling Menéndez to complete his highly successful expedition by capturing and then killing not only the occupants of Fort Caroline but Ribaut's seamen as well. Fortunately a number of paintings made at Fort Caroline by an accomplished French artist named Jacques Le Moyne de Morgues have survived, the earliest existing visual record of French colonization efforts in America.

Already strained by the failure in Canada, French enthusiasm for New World settlement was stilled by the disaster at Fort Caroline. But across the channel, in England, the reign of Queen Elizabeth had commenced, and there was evidence of new interest in the Americas. An account of Ribaut's discoveries and observations published in England in 1563 caused early stirrings of curiosity about the lands and life across the Atlantic.

Among those whose interest was aroused was Sir Humphrey Gilbert, a student of both navigation and military science and a man whose mind was filled with dreams and plans of greater things for England and himself. Sensing an opportunity for England to take a first step toward lessening Spain's New World dominance, he decided to put his ideas in writing for the benefit of his queen. In his "Discourse," written in 1577, he outlined his ideas on how Elizabeth might outfit a fleet of warships under pretense of a voyage of discovery but with the real purpose of cutting off the enemy's profitable trade with Newfoundland and the West Indies.

Technically, at least, England and Spain were at peace, and Queen Elizabeth—only thirty-three years old, yet already eight years into her long reign as monarch—was not yet ready to launch a challenge against her powerful Spanish neighbor. But the time was soon to come, and Gilbert was destined to serve in a major role.

CHAPTER I

The Elizabethans

In any broad assessment of the English effort to colonize North America in the latter part of the sixteenth century the names of Sir Humphrey Gilbert and half a dozen other Elizabethan adventurers come to the fore: Sir John Hawkins, Sir Francis Drake, Sir Martin Frobisher, Sir Richard Grenville, Sir Walter Raleigh, and Simon Ferdinando. Simon who?

This last name must seem strangely out of place in a listing of English explorers. In fact, Simon Ferdinando was Portuguese, born on the island of Terceira in the Azores. A pilot by training and experience, he terminated his allegiance to his native country by entering the service of Spain. His Portuguese name, Simão Fernandes, became Simon Fernandez in Spanish. Subsequently, in English, it was changed again to Simon Ferdinando, or Fernando. Under the flag of Spain he made at least one trip, and probably more, across the Atlantic; then he switched sides once more and became a subject of England.

Ferdinando is credited with being the first to discover a passage from the Atlantic Ocean into the sounds of North Carolina. Thus, on the earliest printed English maps of the southeastern United States, "Port Ferdinando" sticks out incongruously from the multitude of Indian place names. This son of Portugal emerges as the only mariner to play a role in virtually all the earliest serious efforts at

New World settlement by England, first under a crown charter to Gilbert and later under Raleigh.

The record of Ferdinando's early service for Spain is cloudy, but there is no doubt that he spent enough time in American waters to become extremely knowledgeable about the Spanish trade routes. It is likely that he participated in at least one of the expeditions sent out from the West Indies between 1561 and 1573 to explore the coast above Florida, and that it was then that he discovered the Outer Banks inlet to which his name was later applied by the English mapmakers.

Ferdinando's activities in the period from 1573 to 1578, when he turned his back on Spain and entered the service of Queen Elizabeth, are better documented, though his record was not one about which any of his descendants might choose to brag. For during this time, having developed an overt hatred for Spain and things Spanish, Simon Ferdinando turned pirate, roaming the English Channel and the coast of Spain and its mainland neighbors in search of richly laden Spanish vessels. He seems to have found none, and so turned his attention to capturing whatever happened to be at hand, including at least one merchantman under Dutch registry.

On two occasions Ferdinando turned up in England with captured Portuguese vessels as prizes. He got away with it the first time, despite charges by the Portuguese ambassador that Ferdinando had personally killed seven members of the Portuguese crew, but on the second occasion he ended up in an English jail. Again it was the Portuguese ambassador who brought charges of piracy, claiming he had evidence "enough to hang him." By this time, however, it appears that certain men of influence in England were beginning to recognize the advantages of having in the queen's service an experienced navigator possessing intimate knowledge of Spain's West Indies operations.

The charges of piracy brought against Ferdinando by the ambassador of friendly Portugal were too serious to be ignored; but in a classic diplomatic maneuver, the charge was first reduced to suspicion of piracy, and then dropped altogether. It seems no coincidence that Ferdinando was listed at about the same time as having joined the service of Sir Francis Walsingham, the secretary of state and a strong advocate of English ascendancy across the Atlantic.

Walsingham was a power behind the throne in England, equally adept as a designer of broad Elizabethan strategy and as a mover and fixer responsible for implementing such strategy. By the very nature of his position, however, Walsingham was desk bound, and it was thus left to others, the mariners and adventurers later to become known as England's "Sea Dogs," personally to lead foreign expeditions in the name of the queen.

One such leader was Sir Humphrey Gilbert, who had written a discourse in 1577 urging Elizabeth to dispatch a fleet of warships as a means of disrupting Spanish commerce with the New World. Gilbert had to wait a year for his pleas to be answered, and in the process his ideas seemed to mellow. No longer was he calling for outright attacks on Spanish shipping as a means of reducing Spain's foreign influence; rather, he was now proposing the establishment of a permanent English settlement in America to serve as a base of operations against Spain, but well beyond Spanish Florida. And once again Simon Ferdinando's role comes into focus.

In June, 1578, Gilbert received a charter from Queen Elizabeth authorizing and encouraging him to "discover, search, find out, and view such remote heathen and barbarous lands, Countries, and territories, not actually possessed of any Christian Prince or people." This meant America.

Gilbert's first step was to put together a fleet of ten vessels. One of them, the *Falcon*, was a ship of 100 tons, command of which Gilbert gave to his young half-brother, Walter Raleigh. The master and pilot of *Falcon* was Simon Ferdinando.

From the outset it proved to be a disastrous venture. Gilbert was a soldier, not a sailor, and his lack of maritime experience and his difficulty in understanding and dealing with things nautical and with seafarers, especially with seafarers, resulted in serious delays. It was November before the fleet departed English waters, and, according to Gilbert's biographer, David Beers Quinn, it was not long before most of the vessels had "embarked on their normal trade of piracy in home waters," while the rest were forced to turn back to an Irish port for repairs and replenishment of supplies. When once again they put to sea, only *Falcon*, with Raleigh as captain and Ferdinando as pilot, continued on course, calling first at the Canaries and then at the Cape Verde Islands. But that was as far as she went, and by early summer of 1579 even *Falcon* had given up and returned home to England.

Viewed in light of the eventual English success in colonizing North America, the significance of this fruitless effort under Gilbert is that young Walter Raleigh and Simon Ferdinando sailed together for some five or six months, cooped up in a small vessel, sharing daily and sometimes even hourly the responsibility for making decisions concerning the well-being of their vessel and its crew. It was to be Raleigh's destiny never to reach North America, but his dreams of such a venture persisted, and in those dreams he was not soon able to forget the older Portuguese pilot and the exceptional navigational skill and knowledge the man possessed.

Nor, for that matter, was Sir Humphrey Gilbert. Even as Raleigh and Ferdinando were straggling back to England in the *Falcon*, marking an end to Gilbert's initial effort at New World colonization under his royal charter, he and his backers began talking of a second and more ambitious attempt. This time, however, they were determined to exercise more care in planning the expedition, a process which logically called for a preliminary voyage of exploration designed to search out potential sites for settlement.

TO THE RIGHT
WORTHIE AND HONOV-
RABLE, SIR VVALTER RALEGH,
KNIGHT, SENESCHAL OF THE DVCHIES OF

Cornewall and Exeter, and L. Warden of the ftannaries in Deuon
and Cornewall, T.B. wisheth true feliĉtie.

AMORE ET VIRTVTE,

FIGURE I. *Dedication page from Thomas Hariot's* Briefe and
True Report of the New Found Land of Virginia *showing the
coat of arms of Sir Walter Raleigh.*

And who was better qualified to head up such an expedition than the pilot Simon Ferdinando?

For this voyage, Gilbert made available his own frigate, the *Squirrel*, a tiny vessel less than a tenth the size of *Falcon*, but a fast sailer. With a crew of only ten men, Ferdinando departed in March, 1580, made a remarkably rapid passage of the North Atlantic, apparently explored the coast of New England in search of an appropriate location for an English base, and was back home reporting to Gilbert by the end of June.

Ironically, Ferdinando's background and reputation as a pirate and "a ravenous thief" may have been a factor in the unusual dispatch with which this venture was accomplished. Gilbert's backers had serious reservations about sending Ferdinando off by himself, and it was necessary for Sir Humphrey to provide guarantees that the one-time Portuguese corsair would concentrate his efforts on seeking sites for settlement and restrain his natural inclination to go off pirating.

It is not known what plans Gilbert may have had for Ferdinando on his second effort to establish an American colony, since the preparations dragged on for three more years and Ferdinando turned to other pursuits more to his liking. The pilot is known to have made contact with Dr. John Dee, the noted mathematician, astrologer, alchemist, and geographer, and on one occasion provided Dee with a Spanish sea chart of the Atlantic. He also communicated with Captain Martin Frobisher, sending him a letter written in his own hand in English. At that time, Frobisher was preparing for yet another of his expeditions to America under the auspices of the Muscovy Company, which had been formed by London merchants to trade with Scandinavia and Russia, and in his letter Ferdinando offered advice on outfitting vessels for the expedition. Frobisher concentrated his efforts on searching for gold and other precious metals, and when he returned from the Newfoundland area with his ship's hold filled with what turned out to be worthless ore, he lost favor with his backers. Thus when plans were made for an expedition to China and the Pacific, it was Frobisher's lieutenant, Edward Fenton, who was given command. Simon Ferdinando, no doubt tired of waiting ashore for Gilbert to get his second expedition together, signed on with Fenton as copilot of his flagship and thus was not available when Gilbert's flotilla set sail again for America in 1583.

Gilbert's royal charter was designed to provide him with profit and reward if his efforts proved successful, and to induce others to join him. Probably its most significant feature was a provision conferring all the rights of Englishmen at home on those settling in the New World. Gilbert was given broad authority to make and enforce laws, so long as they conformed as much as possible with those in force back in England, and to defend against any attempts to challenge his claim, "as well by Sea as by land." Under a provision empowering him to dispose of land near settled areas, he issued several deeds, some for only a few hundred acres and one for something like two million acres— all in lands he had never seen, let alone settled.

The fleet he put together for his second attempt to reach America consisted of five vessels, ranging in size from the little ten-ton frigate or pinnace *Squirrel*, in which Ferdinando had made his earlier voyage, to the two-hundred-ton *Raleigh*, owned by Walter Raleigh, though Raleigh himself did not sail on her. Queen Elizabeth had reservations about Gilbert's ability to command such a flotilla, reportedly referring to him as "a man of not good happ by sea." But she bowed to his enthusiasm and asked only that he provide her with a portrait of himself before taking leave.

Typically the business of preparing the ships and putting together the company of some 260 men took longer than anticipated. Typically, also, Gilbert's impatience to get started resulted in his decision to try to leave Southampton harbor in the late fall, which would have placed the flotilla out on the North Atlantic in the dead of winter. Fortunately this effort was foiled by bad weather and ill winds, and departure was delayed until the early summer of 1583.

The northern passage brought them to Newfoundland instead of the eventual destination more to the south. Here, where hardy European fishermen had been plying their trade for decades, Gilbert found no less than thirty-six fishing vessels, fairly evenly divided among Spanish, Portuguese, French, and English. These were working men, not diplomats or warriors or statesmen; so they had long since devised a logical and practical method of conducting their fishing operations in peace and harmony. Since the activity was carried on only in the summer months, it had become the accepted practice for the first arrival each year to establish headquarters on shore and for the captain of that vessel to serve throughout the season as a sort of head of government, someplace between a host and a governor. They followed certain accepted rules of procedure, and when a dispute arose, the various parties formed a council to adjudicate the matter. In this way the control of the informal government was rotated on an annual basis among representatives of the various nations.

Gilbert also found that the fishermen had planted crops on shore and that they secured fresh supplies of meat from an off island where early Portuguese fishermen had turned loose some cattle, which apparently had multiplied and flourished. To solidify England's overall claim to these northern territories, established first by John Cabot more than eighty years earlier, Gilbert again planted the flag of England and presided over a ceremony defining England's and his own dominion over the area by virtue of his royal charter.

Any serious attempt to establish a permanent base during the course of the 1583 visit was thwarted by a combination of bad luck, which had already resulted in the loss of two of the five vessels, and the lateness of the season.

Worse was yet ahead, however, for as Gilbert's vessels cruised the nearby islands preparatory to the departure for England, a violent storm, described by some as the worst they had ever encountered, struck the area. For some reason, Gilbert had left his larger flagship and was on board his own little vessel, *Squirrel*, when the tempest arose. At one time he was seen from the larger vessel, seated on the stern, reading aloud from a favorite book, and was reported to have shouted above the shrill wind a prophetic epithet: "We are as neere to heaven by sea as by land." That night *Squirrel* sank beneath the waves, with Gilbert and all hands lost.

Back home in England during that winter of 1583–84, Gilbert's heirs and successors considered yet another attempt to establish an American colony under the authority of his charter. But the document itself was about to expire and the effort was abandoned, leaving the way clear for someone else to take up where Gilbert had failed. That someone else was his younger half-brother, Walter Raleigh, not yet knighted but already well thought of by Queen Elizabeth and Walsingham and others in positions of power. On March 25, 1584, just a few weeks before the expiration date of Gilbert's charter, a new one was issued to Raleigh. Copied largely from Gilbert's, it excluded only the Newfoundland area from the "remote heathen and barbarous Lands, Countries, and territories" he was authorized to search out and settle.

CHAPTER 2

Amadas and Barlowe

Raleigh's plans were well advanced and the vessels of his first expedition were being made ready for sea by the time Queen Elizabeth signed his charter. Only a little more than a month later, on April 27, 1584, his explorers departed for the voyage to America. Master Philip Amadas was aboard the flagship of the two-vessel fleet, and appears to have been in overall command. Master Arthur Barlowe, captain of the second and smaller vessel, was responsible for keeping an accurate record of where they went and what they saw and for preparing a detailed report for Raleigh upon their return to England.

The pilot for the Amadas and Barlowe expedition was a familiar figure in the annals of New World exploration: Simon Ferdinando. This time, however, instead of heading straight across the North Atlantic toward Newfoundland and Labrador, Ferdinando laid a course for the West Indies. He raised land on June 10 and brought the vessels to anchor in a secluded harbor off the coast of a large island, probably Puerto Rico. Remaining there in the very midst of Spanish territory only long enough for the men to replenish their supply of fresh water and food, he then sailed northwest among the islands of the Bahamas, successfully evading Spanish shipping, and on July 4 sighted the North American mainland. Raleigh's explorers had arrived at Ferdinando's destination, the present-day Carolina coast.

Barlowe reported that they sailed northward along the

coast for a distance of 120 English miles before finding
"any entrance, or river, issuing into the Sea." One can
imagine their pent-up excitement over the prospect of being the first Englishmen to land and take possession of
this unclaimed coast. But the experienced Ferdinando was
well aware of the dangerous and ever-shifting underwater
sand shoals rimming the Outer Banks islands. He no
doubt kept lookouts posted at all times, scanning the horizon for breaks in the low-lying coast that would indicate
the existence of inlets. It is also probable that whenever a
potential entry was sighted, he sent the shallow-draft pinnace toward shore for a closer look, a time-consuming
operation that would account for its taking some nine
days to cover the 120 miles before reaching his Port Ferdinando.

We know nothing of Arthur Barlowe's expertise as a
mariner, but there can be no doubt that he was a man of
letters, gifted of word and phrase, and well able to convey
in simple yet dramatic language a fascinating picture of
the lands and people of America. Yet a note of caution is in
order, for he undoubtedly knew that Raleigh intended to
use his report as an inducement for others to join in the
colonization effort. Barlowe was, in short, America's first
English-language publicist, and he must be forgiven if he
sometimes seemed carried away with enthusiasm over
New World bounties, while neglecting to comment on
anything that might convey an unfavorable impression.

Barlowe, as they approached land: "We found shole
water, which smelt so sweetely, and was so strong a smell,
as if we had bene in the midst of some delicate garden,
abounding with all kind of odoriferous flowers."

Barlowe, describing the sand bank on which they landed
and took possession for the queen: "Wee viewed the lande
about us . . . so full of grapes, as the very beating, and
surge of the Sea overflowed them, of which we founde
such plentie . . . that I thinke in all the world the like
aboundance is not to be founde."

Barlowe, on firing a gun as he and his companions stood

on a sand hill overlooking a forested valley: "Such a flocke of Cranes . . . arose under us, with such a crye redoubled by many Ecchoes, as if an armie of men had showted all together."

Barlowe, on wildlife: "This Island had many goodly woods, full of Deere, Conies, Hares, and Fowle . . . in incredible aboundance." On trees: "The highest and reddest Cedars of the world." On the native Indians: "Very handsome, and goodly people, and in their behaviour as mannerly, and civill, as any of Europe."

Identification of the exact spot where Simon Ferdinando first set captains Amadas and Barlowe ashore on the North Carolina coast—the site of a ceremony in which the present United States was first claimed for England—has been the subject of much speculation. The plain truth, however, is that no one knows for sure, and it is a reflection on some highly regarded historians that they purport to have pinpointed the location on the basis of what can only be called circumstantial evidence and scholarly guesswork.

Some maintain that the landing was made on Wococon (Ocracoke); others, that it was on the north end of present-day Hatteras; still others, that it was directly opposite Roanoke Island. Some would-be historians have tried to build a case to prove that the landing was made near Cape Lookout, ignoring all contrary evidence in the process. Those who contend that it was made at Trinity Harbor, approximately where the town of Southern Shores is now located, would seem to be on firmer ground, for this does appear as the point of entry on a map entitled *The arrival of the Englishemen in Virginia*, published by Theodor de Bry in 1590 in Latin, English, French, and German. The problem is that the map is an engraving, quite probably made by an individual who never left Europe. Though it was based on the work of John White, who produced other maps of the Carolina coast, it is not known to what extent White participated in its preparation, if indeed he participated at all. In short, it is impossible to identify the spot on which the first English flag was planted in America.

Raleigh's explorers spent some six weeks on the Outer Banks of North Carolina during the summer of 1584. By chance they had picked the time of year now recognized as the peak tourist season, from early July until the latter part of August—and they managed to crowd a lot of sight-seeing into their brief stay. Barlowe sounded almost like a tourist, so brimming with enthusiasm was his report to Raleigh.

The explorers were at first wary, remaining at anchor for two full days before they saw "any people of the Coun-trey." On the third day after their arrival three men ap-peared in a small boat, which they beached at a safe dis-tance from the English vessels. One of the Indians then left his companions and walked along the shore until he was directly opposite the nearest ship, a gesture taken by the English to mean that he was prepared to confer with them privately and peacefully. Barlowe then described how "the Pilot of the Admirall, Simon Ferdinando, and the Captaine Philip Amadas, my selfe, and others, rowed to the lande, whose comming this fellow attended, never making any shewe of feare, or doubt."

What courage it must have taken for that lone Indian to wait there on the shore, unarmed and unattended, while these strangely attired alien beings detached themselves from a huge craft many times larger than any Indian canoe he had ever seen and made their way toward him; what foolhardy, trusting courage. But such was the nature of those native American inhabitants of this coast, so often described by the English as barbaric, savage, and heathen.

Standing alone before them there on the sandy beach, the Indian proceeded to deliver a speech. The words were unintelligible to the English, but the thrust was obviously friendly. He was formally welcoming the aliens to his land.

"After he had spoken of many things not understoode by

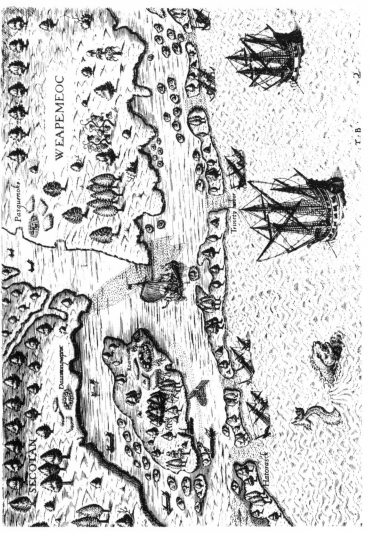

MAP 2. The arrival of the Englishemen in Virginia. *Engraving by Theodor de Bry from a drawing by John White.*

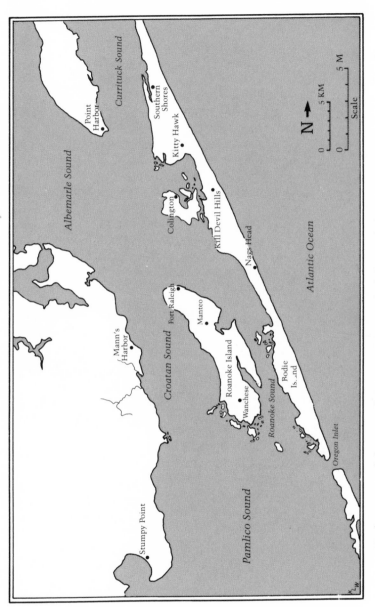

MAP 3. *Modern map of the area shown in* The arrival of the Englishemen in Virginia.

us," Barlowe wrote, "we brought him with his owne good liking, aboord the shippes." They gave him a shirt and a hat and some other presents, and insisted that he taste wine and their meat, "which he liked very well." He was given a tour of both vessels before being rowed back to the point on shore where the welcoming ceremony had taken place. The English, keeping a close watch, then saw him walk down the shore to where his small boat was hidden, but instead of leaving he paddled out into the inlet and started fishing. Shortly—Barlowe said it took only half an hour—he had filled the boat with fish "as deepe as it could swimme" and then returned to shore, where he divided his catch into two equal piles. By gesture he indicated that one pile was for the pinnace and the other for the larger bark; then, having "requited the former benefits receaved, he departed out of our sight."

Imagine the excitement on shore that night when the Indian returned to his village and reported what he had seen. Anxious to see the huge ships and strange men for themselves, others left their village the next morning and crossed the sound in their canoes. In all, some forty or fifty men came to the landing site, led by Granganimeo, brother of the local *weroance*, or chief, Wingina, who was at that time on the mainland recovering from battle wounds.

Again they beached the boats some distance from the English vessels, and again also, as had the lone Indian the day before, Granganimeo and his followers walked along the beach until they were directly opposite the anchored ships. Granganimeo's men then spread a large woven mat on the sand "on which he sate downe, and at the other ende of the matte, foure others of his companie did the like." The remaining Indians stood in the background, some distance from those seated on the mat.

Once more the leaders of the expedition launched a small boat and rowed to shore, their weapons in plain sight. As they landed and walked toward the assembled

Indians, Granganimeo remained seated, as did the four others at the far end of the mat, showing no sign of fear. Granganimeo then beckoned for the English to come forward and sit beside him, which they did. The ceremony of the previous day was repeated, with the Indian delivering a long speech and making, as Barlowe described the scene, "all signes of joy, and welcome, striking on his head, and his breast, and afterwardes on ours, to shewe we were all one, smiling, and making shewe the best hee could, of all love, and familiaritie."

This was the English explorers' first exposure to the social order of the native Americans, who revered their rulers perhaps even more than the English did their own. "The king is greatly obeyed," Barlowe reported, "and his brothers, and children reverenced," adding that "no people in the world carry more respect to their king, Nobilitie, and Governours, then these doe."

None of the Indians standing in the background made a sound while Granganimeo spoke, and not even the four lesser leaders on the far side of the mat spoke aloud, though from time to time they whispered to each other. After giving some presents to Granganimeo, the English distributed gifts to the four other Indian noblemen, but Granganimeo arose and gathered up all the presents, placing them in his own basket. He then lectured them in speech, sign, and pantomime, making it clear "that all things ought to be delivered unto him, and the rest were but his servants, and followers."

This initial meeting with Granganimeo led to a period of extended trade with the natives, large numbers of whom visited the English ships. In exchange for their dressed deer skins the English gave the Indians a variety of merchandise, including such items as copper kettles, though for the most part the trade items were relatively worthless. Barlowe told of one Indian who traded a number of deer skins for a single tin plate, "which he presently tooke up, and clapt it before his breast, and after made a hole in the brimme thereof, and hung it about his necke, making signes, that it would defende him against his enemies arrowes."

Two or three days after the trading began, Granganimeo appeared again and for the first time went aboard the English ships, remaining long enough to dine with the explorers and sample their wine. When next Granganimeo appeared, he was accompanied by his wife, described as "very well favored, of meane stature, and very bashfull," as well as an older daughter and two or three smaller children.

As the trading continued, a "great store of people" visited the vessels, some apparently from villages a considerable distance from the harbor. Leather, coral, and different native dyes were added to the items being bartered, and though the Indians offered premium exchange for hatchets, axes, knives, and swords, the English refused to part with them. They "would have given any thing for swordes," Barlowe said, recounting an instance when Granganimeo offered "a great boxe of pearle" for a sword and some armor. Each day Granganimeo sent the visitors "a brase or two of fatte Bucks" and other meat, as well as fish, melons, and vegetables. On those occasions when he had failed to bring with him enough skins or other items to effect an even trade for desired merchandise, he invariably paid up the next day by sending whatever items had been agreed upon.

The Englishmen soon learned that they were not allowed to trade with other Indians when Granganimeo was present, except those "as weare redde peeces of copper on their heades, like himselfe: for that is the difference betweene the Noble men, and Governours of Countries, and the meaner sort." The Indians took special pains to avert any possible misunderstanding that might lead to a confrontation, especially when they appeared in force. Granganimeo always accomplished this on his visits by having his men go ashore a considerable distance from the ships, where they would light a number of fires, one for each canoe, so that the English "might understand with what strength, and companie, he approached."

Thus were peaceful relationships established between the native Americans and the first Englishmen to visit the North Carolina coast. The time had come, at last, for the Europeans to explore the interior and locate a suitable site for Raleigh's colonization effort.

CHAPTER 3

Roanoke Island

Have you ever noticed how wild animals and birds and fish all seem endowed with some sort of built-in sonar system that enables them to move about at breakneck speeds, in daylight or in total darkness, without colliding with other creatures or obstructions? In flocks of birds or schools of fish, untold numbers move in unison, thousands upon thousands of living creatures, wing to wing or fin to fin, darting this way and that as if welded together into a single entity. Humans, stumbling about in the dim light, have cause for amazement, if not outright jealousy.

But humans, too, possess an instinctive and inbred ability to communicate. Nowhere is this more apparent than when people of one culture and one language first encounter others whose tongue and ways are alien to their own, as was the case when captains Amadas and Barlowe came face to face with Granganimeo and his Indian followers on the Outer Banks of North Carolina in July, 1584.

They dined together, exchanged gifts, and even haggled over the appropriate exchange rate for merchandise they were bartering, all without understanding a single word of each other's language. Obviously this was not a perfect system of communication, and sometimes mistakes were made. Years later, Sir Walter Raleigh wrote that, using sign language, the Spaniards who first visited modern Peru asked the natives the name of the country. In response the Indians pointed to a nearby river and said, "Peru," which actually, according to Raleigh's account, "was either the name of that brooke, or of water in generall."

Raleigh then went on to explain that the same thing had happened with the explorers he sent to the North Carolina coast, "for when some of my people asked the name of that Countrie, one of the Salvages answered *Wingandacon*." Certainly the answer was clear enough, but the problem was that the Indian, able to understand English no better than the Europeans could comprehend the native language, had no idea at all what the question was. He simply responded, courteously, with an offhand comment: "You weare good clothes." Thus was the name *Wingandacon* first applied to England's new lands across the sea.

Despite such difficulties there was a steady improvement in communication, and in time Amadas and Barlowe were able to ask specific questions and receive fairly understandable answers. In this way they began to get a feel for the country around them, a knowledge of the location of rivers and islands and villages, as well as general information on the natural resources of the area and on how the native people lived. Meanwhile, the numerous evidences of goodwill on the part of the Indians finally gave the explorers enough confidence to consider leaving the anchored ships for some firsthand investigation of their own.

For that first cautious exploratory venture they risked only one small boat, with Barlowe and seven others as the sole participants. The destination was Granganimeo's village on the north end of Roanoke Island, some twenty miles from the anchorage. Any concerns Barlowe and his fellow explorers may have harbored as to how they would be received by the natives were put to rest even before they reached the village site, for he reported that Granganimeo's wife "came running out to meete us very cheerefully, and friendly." Granganimeo was absent, but his wife proved to be a most solicitous hostess; she ordered some of the Indian men "to carry us on their backs to the dry ground, and others to bring our oares into the house for feare of stealing."

Undoubtedly, Barlowe was both cautious and curious as he approached the Indian village for the first time. He found that it contained "nine houses, built of Cedar, and fortified round about with sharpe trees, to keepe out their enemies." Barlowe described the largest house as having five rooms, adding that when Granganimeo's wife led them into the main outer room she "caused us to sitte downe by a great fire," while her attendants "tooke off our clothes, and washed them, and dried them againe." As they rested, Barlowe said, "some of the women washed our feete in warme water" while Granganimeo's wife "tooke great paines to see all things ordered in the best manner shee coulde, making great haste to dresse some meate for us to eate."

When their clothes were dry, the eight explorers were led into an interior room, where they discovered a feast spread out on a shelf along the wall, an assortment of roasted and boiled venison and fish, plus melons, fruit, and different kinds of boiled roots.

Part way through his first native meal, no doubt mellowed by the friendly reception, and the bath, and the feasting—and possibly reflecting on his good fortune—Barlowe suddenly caught sight of a group of Indian men armed with bows and arrows entering the enclosure. Others of his men saw them also, and looking "one to wardes another," they cautiously reached for their own weapons. This was a mistake, for Barlowe reported that as soon as Granganimeo's wife "espied our mistrust, she was very much mooved and caused some of her men to runne out, and take away their bowes, and arrowes, and breake them, and withall beate the poore fellowes out of the gate againe."

As evening approached, Granganimeo's wife urged Barlowe and his companions to remain in the village overnight, as her guests, but memories of the incident involving the armed Indians were still fresh in their minds, and they insisted on returning to their boat despite signs of inclement weather. "When we departed in the evening, and would not tarry all night," Barlowe reported, "she was very sorie, and gave us into our boate our supper halfe dressed, pots, and all."

Throughout that night the eight Englishmen remained in their small boat at anchor offshore from the Indian village. Granganimeo's wife, aware of their concern, "was much grieved," Barlowe said, "and sent divers men, and thirtie women, to sitte all night on the bankes side by us . . . using very many wordes to intreate us to rest in their houses."

Rain began to fall, and some of the Indians paddled out to the boat with "fine mattes to cover us from the rayne." But Barlowe refused to return to the village, no matter how cramped, damp, and uncomfortable it was on the boat, "because wee were fewe men, and if wee had miscarried, the voyage had beene in great daunger." He made a point of adding, however, that he was certain there was "no cause of doubt; for a more kinde and loving people, there can not be found in the world, as farre as we have hitherto had triall."

Barlowe's account of this first visit to the Indian village on the north end of Roanoke Island was his only specific mention of where he and his fellow explorers went. It is quite possible that this was the only time Barlowe ventured away from the anchored vessels. But if this is so, he gained considerable knowledge, and much of it amazingly from his personal observations and from discourse with the natives.

His description of the Outer Banks and the sounds and rivers of northeastern North Carolina could as well be made by a modern visitor four hundred years later: "When we first had sight of this Countrey, some thought the first lande we sawe, to be the continent: but after wee entred into the Haven, wee sawe before us another mightie long Sea: for there lieth along the coast a tracte of Islands, two hundreth miles in length, adjoyning to the Ocean sea, and betweene the Islands, two or three entrances."

This, of course, was the string of coastal islands which makes up the Outer Banks, backed up by Pamlico Sound and its tributaries. Within the confines of this "inclosed Sea," Barlowe said there were "about a hundreth Islands of divers bignesses" and he was impressed not only with their beauty, but also with the abundance of flora and fauna in evidence, and the fact that the surrounding waters were filled with "the goodliest and best fishe in the world, and in greatest aboundance."

He spoke of the Indians' "greatest citie," called Skicoak, to the north near modern Chesapeake Bay; of a great body of water to the west of Roanoke Island, our Albemarle Sound; and of the rivers that flowed into it. According to his information the area under the domain of Wingina extended a considerable distance from Roanoke Island, especially to the southwest, where the largest of the Wingandacon settlements was located. This was the village of Secotan, near the shores of the Pamlico River. Beyond Secotan, however, was land Wingina's people considered enemy territory, the "Countrey Neiosioke, situate upon the side of a goodly River called Neus." The inhabitants of Neiosioke were pictured as warlike people, very different from the friendly, peaceful, and innocent natives Barlowe had encountered on and near Roanoke Island.

From the stories he heard, it seemed the Neuse River Indians were forever attacking or planning to attack Wingina's villages, and the resultant wars, "very cruell, and bloodie," were taking a toll. Many of the Indians, he reported, were "marvelously wasted, and in some places, the Countrey left desolate." Intrigued as much with Indian politics and warfare as with their life-style, Barlowe described a time some years earlier when Wingina and the Neiosioke king had put aside their animosity in an effort at permanent coexistence. A feast was arranged in a Neiosioke town, to which a number of Wingina's men and some thirty of his women were invited. But "when they were altogether merrie, and praying before their Idoll," the Neiosiokes suddenly attacked "and slewe them every one, reserving the women and children" only.

On several occasions Wingina's people tried to persuade Amadas and Barlowe to join them in a surprise attack on the Neiosioke town, but the Englishmen refused to be drawn into the fray, uncertain "whether their perswasion be to the ende they may be revenged of their enemies, or for the love they beare to us."

The desire of Wingina's people to have the Europeans join them in an attack on their enemy is quite understandable, for their own weapons were relatively crude and ineffectual. Some of the warriors had swords made of hardened wood; others carried larger wooden clubs, with "the sharpe hornes of a stagge, or other beast" fastened to the end. Unlike the English, they wore no armor, relying instead on "woodden breastplates for their defense." Their primary weapons, and the ones the warriors carried with them at all times, were their bows and arrows. Though the arrows were fashioned from small canes, they were "headed with a sharpe shell, or tooth of a fishe sufficient enough to kill a naked man."

When the Indians went off to war, they carried their idol, of whom, Barlowe said, "they aske counsell." At the same time, he added, "they sing songs as they march to wardes the battell, in steede of drummes, and trumpets."

The Indians were amazed and awed by the guns used by the Englishmen, and whenever one was discharged, Barlowe said, they "would tremble thereat for very feare, and for the strangenes of the same." They seemed equally intrigued with the physical appearance of the visitors, and they "wondred marvelously when we were amongest them, at the whiteness of our skinnes, ever coveting to touch our breastes, and to view the same."

Apparently, however, this was not the first time Indians of Wingandacon had been in contact with white-skinned strangers, for they told a tale of other Indians, residents of the Pamlico area near Secotan, who had discovered some sailors shipwrecked on the coast more than twenty years earlier. In typically friendly fashion the Indians provided the castaways with two of their canoes and helped fasten them together. The white-skinned strangers then made masts to go into their makeshift catamaran and fashioned "sailes of their shirtes, and having taken into them such victuals as the Countrey yeelded, they departed after they had remained in this out Island three weekes."

Not long after the shipwrecked mariners sailed out to sea in their strange and cumbersome little craft, the Indians discovered the two canoes "upon the coast, cast aland in another Island adjoyning," but apparently with no trace of any survivors.

The trusting nature of these native Americans must have been put to the supreme test when Amadas and Barlowe were ready to set sail on the return voyage to England. They invited two men of Wingandacon, later identified as Manteo and Wanchese, to accompany them. Thus Raleigh's explorers took back to England not only an account of their discoveries and samples of commodities they had found on the North Carolina coast but the two natives as well.

CHAPTER 4

The Dawn
of British
Colonialism

The veteran navigator Simon Ferdinando
made another of his rapid and uneventful crossings of the
Atlantic when he piloted the Amadas and Barlowe vessels
on the return voyage from Wingandacon and the North
Carolina coast to England in 1584. Barlowe, apparently
finding nothing noteworthy to mention about the passage,
reported only that the ships "arrived safely in the West of
England, about the middest of September."

News of the return of the two small vessels had been
awaited anxiously throughout the late summer and early
fall by Raleigh and his close associates, and by other influential individuals as well. One of these was Richard
Hakluyt, a scholarly man in his early thirties, trained and
ordained in the ministry, but destined to leave his mark on
England and on the world not as a man of the cloth but as a
geographer and historian.

Orphaned at an early age and raised by a cousin of the
same name, Hakluyt is known today as "Richard Hakluyt, the younger," as distinguished from his older cousin,
who is most often referred to as "Richard Hakluyt, lawyer." The two Richard Hakluyts were named for a common grandfather. Both exhibited a vital interest in geography and exploration, and both expressed in writing their
views on the need for England to wrest from Spain a share
of her near monopoly on American trade and treasure.

Interestingly, both also prepared detailed reports on how Raleigh's venture should be organized and carried forward.

Of the two, however, it is Richard Hakluyt, the younger, who emerges as the man of history, and the one whose name is linked closely with Raleigh's attempts to establish a permanent settlement on Roanoke Island. For more than a quarter of a century the younger Richard Hakluyt filled two key roles in the history of Elizabethan England, for he was both a man about whom history was written and a man who recorded and wrote the history.

During that time he was an active participant in developing plans for American colonization, though it is quite possible he never spent so much as a single night at sea or traveled a greater distance than across the English Channel to France. It is to this preacher-scholar with the confusing name that historians, then and now, have had to turn for the bulk of their knowledge about English exploration and colonization during the exciting age of Elizabeth. Few other individuals, before or since, have single-handedly searched out, compiled, and published such a voluminous mass of basic historical material.

Hakluyt's method was simple. While others were talking about voyages being undertaken or already completed or writing personal letters back and forth, he devoted much of his life to a single tenacious effort to put in writing the full and factual record of Elizabethan England's involvement in the New World. He began by making personal contact with the commanders of the expeditions, the Hawkinses, and Drakes, and Frobishers, and with the captains of their vessels, though regrettably he seems to have missed the intriguing Portuguese pilot with the anglicized Spanish name, Simon Ferdinando. It is not difficult to picture this man of the cloth and of books mingling on the crowded docks of busy English ports with pirates and privateers, with Sea Dogs and seamen, searching for the logs of their vessels, copying their reports, or rapidly scribbling notes as those unable to write poured forth their stories of adventure and hardship.

The resultant massive published work was titled *The Principall Navigations, voiages and Discoveries of the English Nation*. It is the primary source for most of what we now know of these efforts, including the several voyages sent out by Raleigh.

The other side of Hakluyt, the maker-of-history side, emerged even before he began compiling his massive chronicle of adventure. He was a supporter of Gilbert's ill-fated efforts to colonize North America and seems to have had little difficulty turning his attention and his enthusiasm to the even more ambitious project envisioned by young Walter Raleigh. Further, he had clear and definite ideas why such an effort should be considered and how it should be undertaken, and he decided to put those thoughts in writing.

Even as Barlowe and his seven companions were cautiously exploring the Carolina sounds in their small boat and partaking of the hospitality of Granganimeo's wife at the Indian village on Roanoke Island, Hakluyt was hard at work preparing a secret report at Raleigh's request. The resultant document, referred to by modern historians as Hakluyt's *Discourse of Western Planting*, seemed intended primarily for a single purpose—to convince Queen Elizabeth that she should give more than lip service in support of the Raleigh venture.

The *Discourse* contained extensive lists of equipment, supplies, and trained personnel considered necessary for successful colonization, a sort of checklist of what to pack for the trip. Even more important, the extensive arguments presented in an effort to show the queen just how the crown would benefit from the planting of colonies in America can be seen as almost a handbook for successful British colonialism anywhere in the world.

Hakluyt obviously knew his queen—and her idiosyncrasies and special interests. His arguments appealed to three areas of interest—solidifying Queen Elizabeth's power, filling her pocketbook, and spreading the Protestant doctrine. But they went far beyond these basics to deal with such diverse problems as England's sagging economy and foreign trade, her high rate of unemployment, and even the treatment of orphaned children. They dealt extensively with the national defense and the vexing questions of how to induce men to serve in the military and of what to do with them in peacetime when they became jobless or disabled veterans.

The questions raised by Hakluyt, if not the answers, would find a responsive audience among modern monarchs and heads of state. Who could refute his argument, then or now, that the stability of the empire, and in fact of the entire world, was threatened by the continuing rise to power and wealth of a single nation, in this instance King Philip's Spain? Hakluyt suggested that England expand on John Cabot's early claim to English sovereignty over the North American mainland by establishing well-fortified and self-sufficient settlements along the coast and attack Philip's West Indies treasure ships as they sailed back to the Spanish homeland. His specific proposal was to build two or three strong forts adjacent to good harbors at intervals between Florida and Cape Breton, from which attacks could be launched as the treasure ships were borne northward by the Gulf Stream current.

Hakluyt was one of the best-informed geographers of his day, and he used his understanding of the geography of both sides of the Atlantic in a convincing manner. The Carolina coast, he rightly argued, was in the same general latitude as the Mediterranean, and thus was accessible to ocean-going craft "at all times of the yere." This compared favorably with areas further south, where, he claimed, "there is no passage in sommer by lacke of windes," and with those far to the north, which are so adversely affected in winter "by yse and extreme colde."

He envisioned vast agricultural enterprises, including the "planting of vines and olive trees" and the resultant production of "wyne and oyle." Oranges, lemons, and "figges" were among the commodities to be produced, as well as more conventional crops. The vast forests of oak and pine and cedar contained "plentie of excellent trees for mastes," thus making possible a major shipbuilding industry. Beyond that, the pine forests would provide a ready source for much-needed naval stores, including "pitche" and "tarr," natural products which in fact were later to become the foundation of the North Carolina economy.

To provide cheap labor in the overseas settlements some of England's multitude of unemployed workers could be transported to the new land, thus easing a serious problem in the home country, which Hakluyt described as "swarminge at this day with valiant youthes rusting and hurtfull by lack of employment." Debtors would be released from prison and given a new chance abroad, and even the destitute orphans could be shipped to America and trained in the crafts, thus becoming grateful and loyal subjects of England. As for the veterans, they could be employed both in defending the settlements and instructing others in the military arts, thus creating a large and well-trained reserve force upon which the motherland could call in time of national emergency. And a vastly expanded merchant fleet, composed mostly of large vessels designed and built in America for the transatlantic trade, would be available to double as ships of war when needed.

Nowhere in his treatise was Hakluyt more eloquent than when he donned his pastoral robes and expounded on the unique opportunity that American colonization would provide for advancing the cause of Protestantism. The natives, he asserted, were an untapped source of converts, and the land they occupied, once pacified, would be an ideal sanctuary for Protestant refugees from the Continent. Citing the murder of Spanish friars in Florida by hostile Indians as an example of the dangers that awaited ill-prepared missionaries, he conceded that converting a continent full of "idolaters" would be risky. But he justified the risks with a quote from the Apostle Paul, who had himself taken considerable risks to spread the faith: "Whosoever shall call on the Lorde shall be saved: But howe shall they call on him in whom they have not beleved? And howe shall they beleve in him of whom they have not hearde? And howe shall they heare withoute a preacher? and howe shall they preache excepte they be sent?" And he insisted that if his fellow clergymen would learn the language and customs of the Indians, treat them civilly, and use common sense in their comings and goings, they might "with discrecion and myldenes distill into their purged myndes the swete and lively liquor of the gospell" without exposing themselves to undue hazard.

Of course, Hakluyt realized that converting the Indians and providing "a sure place to receave people from all partes of the worlde that are forced to flee for the truthe of gods worde" would do far more than simply ensure the advancement of "sincere relligion." He proposed that the establishment of a strong Protestant colony in North America protected by a buffer of Indians loyal to the Defender of the Faith, Queen Elizabeth, would help subvert Spanish rule throughout the New World, for he was convinced that exposure to Protestantism and a liberal dose of English "humanitie, curtesie, and freedome" would cause the subjugated Indians in Florida and elsewhere to "revolte cleane from the Spaniarde."

Hakluyt shared with many of his contemporaries the belief that there existed an as yet undiscovered passage through the North American continent which would provide English vessels with a direct and much shorter route from Europe to China. Efforts to locate this Northwest Passage would stand a much better chance of success, he reasoned, if the exploring vessels could be based at one of Raleigh's proposed settlements on the coast of North America instead of at English ports on the other side of the Atlantic.

The exact date when Hakluyt's *Discourse* was delivered

to Queen Elizabeth is not known. It seems certain that he did not complete it until after Amadas and Barlowe had returned from their voyage of exploration to Ferdinando's port on the Carolina coast. The logical assumption is that Hakluyt wanted to talk with one or both of the captains personally so he could have firsthand information on conditions in that part of America before completing his document.

Meanwhile, other pressures were being brought to bear on the queen. The elder Hakluyt, "Richard Hakluyt, lawyer," was compiling his own set of inducements for royal support of such a venture. Others, never identified, were engaged in preparing similar lists. In different parts of England various individuals with special experience and talent were being encouraged to join with Raleigh and take part in the forthcoming expedition. One result of all this was that there was so much activity along the Thames waterfront that officials of Philip's government in Spain were expressing concern over what was taking place. Overall, there appears to have been a widespread understanding, as historian Quinn later stated, that this venture of Raleigh's "was the first serious attempt to transport Englishmen overseas to settle in America."

In November or early December a bill was introduced in Parliament to further confirm Raleigh's patent from Queen Elizabeth. How much this action was designed to publicize the venture or to influence the queen is not known, but the bill was assigned to a special committee heavily stacked with prominent supporters of North American colonization. These included Sir Francis Drake, who was even then preparing for yet another expedition against the Spanish Indies; Sir Philip Sidney, one of Drake's staunchest supporters; Sir Francis Walsingham, an active backer of Raleigh; and Sir Richard Grenville, who was to take direct command of the 1585 Raleigh expedition.

The bill pointed out that, as a result of the "Labor &

procurement of the said Walter Rawleigh," there had been discovered "a Land called Wyngandacoia, not inhabited by anye Christian Prince or Christian people." This was the first such successful effort on the American mainland after several previous attempts, and considerable information on the advantages of establishing an English settlement in Wingandacon had been compiled by the explorers. Specific mention was made of extensive intelligence obtained from the two Indians, described in the bill as "some of the people borne in those partes brought home into this our Realme of England." This seems a clear indication that Manteo and Wanchese had learned enough of the English language, and their tutor or tutors enough Algonkian, to communicate readily.

Opposition to the bill developed in the House of Commons over a provision that would have enabled Raleigh to remove prisoners from English jails and transport them to America and another which would have given him authority to impress ships and sailors. As a result the bill was withdrawn before final action could be taken, though failure to pass the legislation seems to have had little effect on preparations for the expedition.

By early spring of 1585 a fleet of seven vessels had been assembled in Plymouth, under command of Grenville. An experienced military man, Captain Ralph Lane, had been relieved of duty in Ireland so he could join the expedition. Simon Ferdinando was signed on as the pilot. Several members of Parliament, including Thomas Cavendish, had joined Grenville, and a number of artisans, craftsmen, soldiers, and sailors were preparing to make the voyage.

Despite Hakluyt's *Discourse* and the best efforts of Raleigh and his cadre of influential supporters, Queen Elizabeth had shied away from becoming a full partner in the undertaking, but she did give limited support in several different ways. As a token of her interest in the venture—and in Raleigh—she permitted him to change the name of Wingandacon to Virginia, in honor of herself, the Virgin

Queen of England, and on January 6, 1585, bestowed knighthood on Raleigh. She also provided a large vessel as flagship of the fleet and authorized Raleigh to secure a sizable quantity of gunpowder from the royal stockpile.

At long last the dawn of British colonialism was at hand.

CHAPTER 5

Grenville's 1585 Expedition

In April, 1585, for the second successive spring, Raleigh's vessels departed the coast of England bound for the North American mainland. The specific destination, North Carolina's Outer Banks and Roanoke Island, erroneously called Wingandacon by Amadas and Barlowe, had been officially renamed Virginia. But this was not the only name change of note, for Raleigh himself, thirty-three years old and now knighted, would forevermore be known as "Sir Walter."

Compared with the two small craft in which Amadas and Barlowe had sailed the previous year, this seven-vessel fleet commanded by Sir Richard Grenville was a flotilla of substance. The flagship, or "admiral," was Queen Elizabeth's ship, the 160-ton *Tiger*, captained by Grenville. This was the lead ship, the one the others were to follow, and her complement logically included the chief pilot of the expedition, Simon Ferdinando.

Two of the other vessels were owned, wholly or in part, by their captains. One was the 100-ton *Lion*, of which George Raymond was captain and owner; the other was the 50-ton *Elizabeth*, owned and commanded by Thomas Cavendish, a member of the House of Commons, who had been designated by Raleigh as high marshal of the expedition, a position somewhat akin to chief judge.

Raleigh owned the four remaining vessels: the 140-ton *Roebuck*, with John Clarke as captain; the 50-ton *Doro-*

thy, possibly commanded by Arthur Barlowe; and two smaller pinnaces which tagged along as tenders for the larger craft.

Unfortunately this bare outline of basic information on the composition of the Grenville fleet, this simple listing of vessels by name and tonnage and captain, is all that Richard Hakluyt gave us in his published narrative concerning the vessels and men and cargo that made up the 1585 expedition. But this was no voyage of exploration, for Grenville's instructions and intent were to locate an appropriate base on the fringe of Spanish Florida, build a fort, and establish a permanent colony; so it is important to look elsewhere for information about the makeup of this expeditionary force.

Normally we would turn to the great archives of Europe and the British Isles, for stashed away in those depositories are the records of innumerable voyages and voyagers. The ancient documents found there, usually still legible despite the passage of time, are the fount from which flows our knowledge of sixteenth- and seventeenth-century exploration and the early colonization of America. For many expeditions there are shipping lists and bills of lading, which provide information on exactly what cargo was carried and just how much there was of each particular item, right down to the last ounce or pint. There are plans of vessels, drawn to precise scale, and inventories of equipment and supplies; and there are lists of crewmen and passengers, and even of the clothes they wore, the food they ate, and the beer and water they drank.

Alas, the principals in the 1585 venture—Raleigh, Grenville, Ferdinando, Lane, Cavendish, and Raymond—left us none of this. In such instances the historian must turn detective, following one lead after another, clue after clue, in his search for facts on which to base conclusions. Owing to the tenacious effort of one modern historian, David Quinn, bits and pieces of information about preparations for the expedition have been brought to light with which to try to fill in the blanks. Foremost among his discoveries is a series of anonymous notes, almost certainly prepared for Raleigh and Thomas Cavendish, containing detailed advice on the types of individuals who should be enlisted for the venture and the nature and quantity of the equipment and supplies they should carry with them. Combining these with the lists in the appendix to Hakluyt's *Discourse*, we can get a good idea of what might have been planned, if not actually prepared, for the undertaking.

The notes proposed a force of eight hundred armed men as the nucleus of the colony to be "planted" in Virginia. This was in addition to the sailors needed to man the vessels, the officers and leaders of the expedition, and the various artisans and specialists. Half of the eight hundred soldier-colonists would be armed with guns. Of the remainder, one hundred and fifty would have longbows; one hundred, swords; another one hundred (wearing light armor), pikes; and the remaining fifty, more fully armored, battle axes.

Soldiering was only one of several essential jobs to be assigned to these eight hundred men. As soon as a site could be selected for a settlement, two hundred would be sent out on trips lasting eight to ten days to explore the surrounding country. The remaining six hundred would be put to work building a fort, an activity in which five hundred of them would be engaged at all times while the remaining one hundred stood guard. Assignments to the work force, guard duty, and exploration would be rotated until such time as the fort was completed.

The commander of this military force was to be given the rank of general. Serving under him would be a colonel, a sergeant major, captains, two justices, and a high treasurer, as well as a number of other individuals with training and experience in specific fields. Among these were an engineer, a geographer, a painter, a surveyor, an apothecary, an alchemist (to test minerals), a lapidary (or specialist in precious stones), plus a number of carpenters, masons, makers of mud walls, miners, and, of course, husbandmen to do the farming.

In his *Discourse*, Hakluyt went into much more detail and expanded greatly on the list of proposed participants in such a venture. He suggested including, as backup for the military force, men trained in making everything from gunpowder, saltpeter, and light shields to spades, shovels, and the heavy baskets that would be used for carrying dirt while a fort was being built. He even said there should be one man with expertise in making eyelet holes.

Hakluyt felt it would be necessary to build craft especially designed for use on the American sounds and rivers—"swifte boates and barges" is the way he described them, "to passe by winde and oare"—so he called for the inclusion of shipwrights, oar makers, and "makers of Cable and Cordage." As a "defence againste shott from the shoare" he advised that these small craft should be covered with heavy, quilted canvas.

Hakluyt seems to have made a determined effort to anticipate every conceivable need that might arise in an American colony, so he proposed taking along specialists in finding springs and sinking wells, plus others experienced in such diverse activities as making nets; planting sugarcane, grapevines, and olive trees; burning ashes for soap and making barrels in which to ship the soap ashes; and even one person, a "burrachiomaker," whose job was to make leather bottles for the wine that would be produced from grapes to be raised in the vineyards. The list did not end there, for the expedition was to include individuals involved in more conventional pursuits—blacksmiths, cobblers, tanners, dressers of chamois, pail makers, bottle makers, barbers, tailors, launderers, fishermen, hunters, bakers and brewers, tile makers, lime makers, bricklayers, lath makers, and experts in weaving reeds, rushes, and broom straw.

Had the Hakluyt recommendations been followed, one or more of the Grenville vessels would have had a close resemblance to Noah's Ark. He called for taking a variety of livestock, including male and female hogs, deer, chickens, ducks, and turkeys. Of special importance were the dogs, three different kinds of dogs, each for a specific purpose: greyhounds "to kill deere &c"; mastiffs "to kill heavie beastes" and to keep watch at night; and bloodhounds "to recover hurte deere."

Heading the list of foodstuffs to be carried were "hoggs fleshe barrelled and salted, in great quantitie" and beef "barrelled in lesse quantitie." These were to be supplemented by such staples as fish meal, oatmeal, rice, butter, cheese, honey, dried beans, peas, prunes and olives, and "vinegar very stronge." For liquid refreshment there should be Canary wines, brewed beer, and "Syders of ffrance, spaine, and England."

The need to plant gardens was not overlooked. The lists contained the names of numerous seeds, such as turnip, radish, carrot, "garlicke," onion, cucumber, cabbage, parsley, lettuce, thyme, rosemary, and mustard. Obviously salads, properly seasoned, were to be a staple of the settlers' diet, for in addition to the seeds Hakluyt's list called for ample supplies of salad oils.

To what extent Raleigh and Grenville followed these recommendations cannot be known for sure, but there are strong indications that the initial preparations were for a force and a fleet much larger than that which finally departed Plymouth in April, 1585.

Difficulty in securing enough vessels, and especially in locating the appropriate types of vessels, may have brought about a gradual reduction of the size and scope of the venture. In the fall of 1584, not long after Hakluyt's *Discourse* was delivered to the queen, there was a report that sixteen vessels were being readied for the voyage to Wingandacon in America. At that time in various parts of England, and in the Spanish halls of government as well, the name *Wingandacon* was being used more and more frequently, though the spelling of England's proposed base in America took a wide variety of forms, ranging from

Wyngandecora to *Wingantekoy* to *Wingane Dehoy* to *Wingan deCoy*.

There were reliable reports at about that time that Raleigh, trying to put together a fleet of sufficient size to accomplish his goals, sent one or more of his own vessels on privateering voyages during the fall and winter, and it appears that at least one prize, and possibly as many as three, had been taken. Even so, by mid-winter the proposed sixteen-vessel force had been reduced to thirteen, and a spring departure was being spoken of.

By the time the fleet took leave of the homeland the number had been further reduced to seven vessels, and it can be assumed that similar reductions had been made in the number of men involved. Obviously it would have taken a much larger complement of seamen to handle sixteen vessels properly, or even thirteen, than it did to make up the crews of *Tiger* and her six consorts. Also Grenville's five ships and two small pinnaces provided much less room for the soldiers and colonists, and for their supplies and equipment, than there would have been on a fleet twice that size or larger.

The best indications are that Grenville set sail with about six hundred men, about evenly divided between soldier-colonists and mariners. Among those taking part were several who had been on the Amadas and Barlowe voyage of exploration and discovery the previous year, including Philip Amadas himself, who had been designated admiral of the fleet and was thus second in command to Grenville. Arthur Barlowe apparently occupied a lesser role, but Simon Ferdinando, as chief pilot, was once again responsible for getting them to their destination safely.

Details about the voyage from England to America, which took less than a month, are sketchy at best. Ferdinando planned to follow the customary route, sailing south from Plymouth along the coast of France, Spain, Portugal, and Africa until he reached the latitude of the Canary Islands, then turning almost due west for the long ocean passage to the West Indies. On the very first leg of the voyage, however, the fleet ran into bad weather. As the velocity of the wind increased and the storm became a raging fury, one of the smaller vessels, the pinnace serving as *Tiger's* tender, swamped and sank. Soon it became impossible to maintain visual contact with the other vessels, and the fleet was scattered, leaving *Tiger* to continue alone in the hope that the others might be able to follow and in time catch up with the flagship.

Ferdinando set a course for Dominica in the Leeward Islands, arriving there on May 7. He then made his way in a northwesterly direction through the Caribbean, passing close to St. Croix in the Virgin Islands and finally reaching his destination on the southern coast of Puerto Rico. Almost certainly this was the same harbor in which Ferdinando had paused briefly a year earlier to take on water. Called the "Baye of Muskito" by the English, it is identified by Quinn as the present-day Tallaboa Bay.

None of the other vessels had reached the Muskito Bay rendezvous when *Tiger* dropped anchor offshore, and Grenville faced a crucial decision. Should he remain at anchor there, waiting for stragglers from his fleet to show up? And if so, for how long, since this was established Spanish territory, both ashore and afloat? Or should he send in his military expert, Captain Ralph Lane, with a sufficiently large work crew to erect temporary fortifications? Apparently the loss of *Tiger's* tender, the pinnace, in the storm off the coast of Portugal was a key factor in his final decision, since it would have been almost impossible for him to explore the sounds back of the Outer Banks, or reach Roanoke Island, without such a craft. Lane was ordered ashore to fortify Muskito Bay.

The nerve of those Elizabethans. After nearly a hundred years of Spanish occupation of the West Indies—of that very island, in fact—they had anchored their single vessel and sent most of their men ashore to construct a fort. And they intended to remain there, in the very heart of Spanish America, for however long it might take them to build and launch an ocean-going craft.

FIGURE 2. *Sir Richard Grenville (courtesy of the North Carolina Division of Archives and History).*

CHAPTER 6

In the Spanish Indies

The name most often associated with the attempts to establish England's first permanent New World colony in the 1580s is that of Sir Walter Raleigh, and rightfully so. But if there is a hero in this story, it is not Raleigh, nor is it one of his knighted associates, Sir Richard Grenville or Sir Francis Drake. Rather, it is a relatively obscure individual named John White—artist and author, commander and governor, yet a man who is best remembered as a distressed and heartbroken father and grandfather, tirelessly searching for a group of men, women, and children who were to become known as the lost colonists of Roanoke Island. But that was later.

In May, 1585, when Grenville's *Tiger* arrived at Puerto Rico, there can be no question that White was aboard, though his name is hardly mentioned among those participating in the expedition. Yet John White was there—John White the artist—for he left a series of exceptional watercolor drawings as a permanent record of what he saw at Muskito Bay; drawings so detailed that they add substance and feeling and understanding to the brief written reports of what Grenville's men did there.

The journal of the *Tiger* states only that "the most part of our companie landed, and began to fortifie" an area located "very neere to the sea side" and bounded on one side by a river and on the other two by woods and swamp. White's drawing of the site pictures the fort and surrounding area as if from on high and provides illuminating detail to fill in the blank spots left by the brief written account. He even provided a scale of paces from which it is possible to measure the surprisingly large area enclosed by the fortification—more than three hundred feet across in each direction.

It can be assumed that Ralph Lane, the military man, designed and supervised construction of the fortification. Planning the defensive works was tricky business, for protection had to be provided not only against a possible attack from the sea but against one from the interior as well, since the Englishmen were well aware that a Spanish base was located a relatively short distance away.

Lane's approach was to take advantage of natural features, most notably a small river flowing into the sea on the west side of the proposed site, plus a dense swamp on the northeast side. He connected these by throwing up lines of earthworks, broken by bastions or gun positions from which his men could command the approaches. Manning shovels in the tropical heat and under constant attack from hordes of mosquitoes, the hundreds of men doing this work were forced to dig deep enough to strike water, thereby creating a double line of defense—a high earthwork and a moatlike ditch.

With the enclosure thus protected on all sides by the swamp, the river, the earthworks, and the moats, Lane left a large area of uncleared forest in the middle, possibly to provide cover for his sharpshooters in the event that the outer line of defenses was breached. Lane's own encampment was within the enclosure, on the north side. White's drawing shows two Spanish horses nearby, captured on the island. The horses were confined in a paddock adjacent to the swamp, with a guarded position not too far away.

Grenville's base of operations, the "General's Quarters," was on the south side, near the beach. It was here that the pinnace was being constructed, and the vessel appears in White's drawing, as yet undecked and without masts, but with timbers in place. Shipbuilders are pictured also, drilling holes and performing other tasks, and a large fire nearby could have been for a forge.

All of the timber for the pinnace, which was probably thirty feet or so in length and designed to carry at least twenty tons of cargo, was cut as much as three miles from the fort and hauled through the forest on wheeled carriages. White shows one such vehicle, pulled by about a dozen men, with a number of others guarding the procession as it emerges from the woods. An accompanying description on the drawing reads: "The manner of drawing in of tymber, into the fort for the buylding of a Pynnes." Even Grenville is shown, astride a horse, approaching the fortification from the other side of the river with a large force of armed men, some of whom are in the process of fording the shallow watercourse.

What were the Spaniards doing while all this was going on? For one thing they were keeping a wary eye on the intruders. On the fourth day after their arrival the English spotted eight soldiers from the nearby base, on horseback, observing the activity from a distance. After half an hour or so, Lane sent out ten marksmen, but the Spaniards galloped off as they approached.

Meanwhile, *Tiger* remained anchored well offshore, partly sheltered by a small island, with a lookout constantly posted to warn of a Spanish attack from the sea. On May 19, exactly a week after the arrival at Muskito Bay, the man on watch sighted the masts of a ship on the distant horizon, and shortly a formidable craft was observed bearing down on *Tiger's* position. The consternation and excitement aboard Grenville's flagship is easy to imagine. The initial sounding of alarms, the call to quarters for the skeleton crew left on board, a frenzied and frightening time as the lookouts anxiously scanned the surrounding waters to see if the approaching vessel was alone or part of a Spanish squadron. Then, relief! For this was *Elizabeth*, Thomas Cavendish's ship. Separated from *Tiger* three thousand miles away off the Bay of Portugal more than a month earlier, she was at last rendezvousing with her flagship.

Though Grenville did not know it, he had happened to arrive at Muskito Bay at a time when the Spanish garrison at the nearby base was at reduced strength, and while news of the activities of the English was being transmitted back to the headquarters of the Puerto Rican command, the officer in charge of the detachment could do little but keep a watch on what was going on within Lane's fortification. On May 22 he sent out twenty horsemen. These were met by twenty of Lane's men on foot, plus two others mounted on the captured Spanish horses. The *Tiger* journal reports that almost immediately the Spaniards "shewed to our men a flagge of truce, and made signs to have a parle with us." Two of the English soldiers "went halfe of the way upon the sands, and two of theirs came and met them," the journal records. The meeting began in a friendly enough manner, with the Spaniards offering "very great salutations." As soon as these preliminaries were over, however, they launched into a tirade, demanding to know why the Englishmen had landed on Spanish territory, and especially what right they had to build a fort.

The response was straightforward enough. The Englishmen stated that their "principal intention was onely to furnish our selves with water, and victuals, and other necessaries" which were badly needed and that they hoped that these supplies "might be yelded us with faire, and friendly means." If not, the English said, they were fully prepared "to practise force, and to releeve our selves by the sworde." This forthright statement, backed up by the obvious strength of Grenville's garrison, was enough to still the Spanish protests. The meeting ended, according to the report, when the Spaniards "yelded to our requestes with large promises of all curtesie, and great favor, and so our men and theirs departed."

This encounter strengthened Grenville's resolve to finish his business at Muskito Bay and take to the sea again as soon as possible. Work on the pinnace was completed

The text within the drawing reads:

THE 23th of Maye the Generall in his
shyppes arriued at S.t John's Iland where
he fortefied in this manner, loke in this
maner, and sente at Branca. And then
departed from thense the xxiij.th of the
same moneth. 1585.

A fresh ryuer

The Genera[l]

FIGURE 3. John White drawing of the plan of the
fortifications at Muskito Bay (© 1964 The Trustees of the

British Museum; print courtesy of the North Carolina Collection, University of North Carolina at Chapel Hill).

the following day, and the small vessel was hauled to the beach and launched. The Spaniards' "promises of all curtesie" appear to have included one to provide the English with fresh food, and Grenville, "with his Captaines, and Gentlemen," marched that same day some four miles into the interior to a previously agreed upon meeting place. But when the Spaniards, "keeping their old custom for perjurie and breache of promise came not," Grenville set fire to the woods and hurried back to the fort, where he had the woods in and around the enclosure fired also. This done, Grenville and Lane and most of the colonist-soldiers returned to *Tiger.* Putting a small crew aboard the pinnace, the vessels—three of them now, with the return of *Elizabeth* and the construction of the pinnace—weighed anchor and departed Muskito Bay.

It had taken only eleven days to build the fortification, locate, cut, and haul in the timbers for the pinnace, and build the little vessel. The relatively brief layover at Muskito Bay had been a most profitable one for Grenville. Less than two weeks earlier he had arrived with a single vessel, *Tiger.* Now he was departing with a small fleet at his disposal. But problems remained. For one thing he was short of supplies, because the other vessels—*Roebuck, Lion, Dorothy,* and the remaining pinnace—had not yet reached Puerto Rico. Whether any of these would eventually meet him on the Outer Banks, or even whether any of them had survived the Bay of Portugal storm, was unknown. Accordingly, before leaving the West Indies, he resolved to make a good effort at replenishing those supplies which were most scarce, especially salt, and he seemed to have no compunction as to how or where he got them.

Grenville was lucky. The very first night out from Muskito Bay *Tiger* came up on a Spanish frigate, which was captured without resistance; the following day a second Spanish vessel was taken, this one laden with a rich cargo. Since they were at that time close by Cape Rojo on the southwestern tip of Puerto Rico, said to be the best source of salt on the entire island, Grenville dispatched Lane to the cape in one of the captured frigates to get salt. Lane was gone for three days; in that time he somehow managed to land near Cape Rojo, discover two large Spanish salt mounds there, construct a rather formidable earthen fort around them with only about thirty men (including six crewmen from the captured Spanish ship) at his disposal, and load the salt on his vessel.

White must have been a member of the company, for he prepared a detailed watercolor of Lane's salt fort, with the three-masted Spanish prize anchored offshore. The fort, in the general shape of a square with pointed bastions protruding from three sides, consisted of earthworks surrounded by a wide ditch, with an opening on the side facing the sea. In White's drawing a small open boat is drawn up out of the water and is being loaded with salt. One man is on guard in each of the bastions, while others are pictured chopping away at one of the salt mounds and carrying bags of it from the mound to the lighter.

White's two drawings of fortifications erected by the English on Puerto Rico, the large one at Muskito Bay and the smaller one at Cape Rojo, provide information otherwise lacking on Grenville's activities in the Spanish Indies. But these were only two of more than thirty watercolors that White made in the Caribbean. The others depicted native creatures and plant life. These exquisitely detailed drawings include a land crab, fireflies and other insects, scorpions, an iguana, an alligator, a Portuguese man-of-war, and a variety of birds, fish, and edible fruits.

White made no drawings of Spaniards, although Lane's salt gathering operation seemed threatened when several of them appeared, some on horseback and others afoot. They "gave him the looking, and gazing on, but durst not come neere him to offer any resistance," according to the written account, and Lane succeeded in loading the salt aboard his frigate and departing before Spanish reinforcements could arrive.

If Grenville was acting within the bounds of accepted

sixteenth-century international law by sending Lane in a stolen Spanish vessel to steal Spanish salt, it appears that he may have stepped over the limits of legality in his next action. He sailed to the island of Hispaniola and brought the five vessels under his command to anchor right in the middle of the Spanish port of Isabela. His purpose was to exchange the crewmen captured on the Spanish vessels, and the cargoes and possibly even the ships themselves, for needed supplies.

Grenville arrived at Isabela on the first day of June, 1585. Communications were soon established with the Spaniards, several of whom visited *Tiger* and the other vessels, where they were "wel intertained." But Grenville was stalking bigger game; he sent messages to the local governor that there were in his fleet "many brave, and gallant Gentlemen" who would consider it an honor to meet his excellency in person. Two days later the governor arrived, accompanied by "a lusty Frier, & 20. other Spaniards, with their servants, & Negroes." As soon as those on the ships spotted this impressive assemblage, Grenville and most of his officers and "gentlemen," all properly attired for such a meeting, were rowed ashore. What a ludicrous sight there on the sandy beach of the Isabela harbor, as the Spanish governor formally received the English commander, while "the Spanish Gentlemen saluted our English Gentlemen, and their inferiour sort did also salute our Souldiers and Sea men."

At first the Spaniards appeared wary, for they must have been aware of Drake's earlier attacks on their countrymen elsewhere in the islands, but in time "the curtesies that passed on both sides were so great, that all feare and mistrust on the Spanyardes part was abandoned." It was time then for festivities, and the visiting Elizabethans took it on themselves to be the hosts. Grenville's men quickly erected two large "banquetting houses covered with greene boughs," one for "the gentlemen," the other for the servants, and set a sumptuous banquet. Grenville did it up in first-class style, serving the food on his finest silver, accompanied by the sound of trumpets and what was described as a "consort of musick."

So delighted were the Spaniards that they immediately arranged for a large herd of white cattle to be brought down from the nearby mountains, together with horses, one "for every Gentlemen and Captaine that woulde ride," already saddled. They then turned loose three of the cattle, and for several hours the Spanish and English gentry rode together in friendly sporting competition. When at last the chase was ended, the two groups exchanged "many rare presents and gifts" and made arrangements to meet again the following day to engage in serious barter and trade.

From the standpoint of the English, at least, the Isabela venture was as successful as anyone could have hoped. They received considerable livestock—horses, cattle, goats, swine, and sheep—to take with them to Virginia, plus quantities of bull hides, sugar, ginger, pearl, tobacco, and other commodities, almost certainly to be transported back to England for sale as a means of partly underwriting the investment made by Raleigh and his partners. In exchange, they apparently gave only the commodities they had stolen from other Spaniards a few days earlier in the captured vessels.

Exactly one week after his arrival, Grenville departed Isabela, heading in a general northerly direction through the Bahama Islands, stopping once to hunt seals and another time to search for additional salt. On June 20 the voyagers sighted the coast of Florida, and three days later were almost wrecked on "a breache called the Cape of Feare." The following day they anchored in a protected harbor, probably modern Beaufort Inlet, where they engaged successfully in an activity that today draws hordes of visitors to the area, fishing. Elated at having made a large catch on a single tide, they set sail again and, finally, on June 26, reached their destination—the inlet called Wococon on the North Carolina Outer Banks.

CHAPTER 7

Planting the First Colony

Some people living on the Outer Banks will tell you that the inlet Sir Richard Grenville's colonists referred to as Wococon when they reached the Carolina coast June 26, 1585 is the present-day Ocracoke Inlet. Others say straight out that this is not true. The fact is that both are partly right and partly wrong.

Confused? You should be—unless, that is, you understand how these channels through the Outer Banks are formed and what happens to them, year by year, day by day, even hour by hour.

To begin with, they really are not inlets at all, but outlets. They exist solely to serve as relief valves through which tremendous quantities of water, falling initially as rain in the mountains and piedmont and coastal plain, reach the Atlantic Ocean. Because the amount of rainfall varies widely from season to season the quantity and velocity of the water seeking an outlet to the sea also varies. Consequently, just as new gullies form on the slope of a freshly plowed hill and deposit sediment in low-lying areas after a heavy rain, so also do new channels open and new shoals form with the periodic fluctuations in the flow of water through the Outer Banks openings.

Other factors compound the confusion. Both the storms that deposit excessive amounts of rainwater upstream and those that push ocean water with hurricane force against the low and narrow Outer Banks often cause new inlets to open and old ones to change dramatically in width and depth. Finally, the Outer Banks inlets are migratory; they move gradually from north to south as the littoral drift along this coast causes them to build up on the north side and erode on the south side.

Both Wococon and Ocracoke are identified on contemporary maps as being in the same general location, approximately midway between Cape Hatteras and Cape Lookout, connecting lower Pamlico Sound with the ocean in an area long known as Raleigh Bay. As for the name, the progression from Wococon to Ocracoke was a gradual one, for at various times it was Wokokon, and Wococock, then Ocacock, and Ocracock, before becoming Ocracoke. Whether this one inlet has been open continuously for four centuries nobody knows, but even if it has, the present-day Ocracoke Inlet has almost certainly migrated some distance from Grenville's Wococon.

It was through this Wococon Inlet that Simon Ferdinando attempted to sail the flagship, *Tiger*, three days after the fleet reached the Outer Banks. Four hundred years later experienced coastal captains, at the helms of fishing trawlers similar in size to *Tiger*, but motor driven, aided by beacons and buoys marking the channels, and equipped with such modern aids as depth finders, often have difficulty navigating Wococon's modern sister inlets, and many have wrecked their craft in the attempt. Ferdinando's ship was almost wrecked also. After running hard aground on a Wococon shoal, *Tiger* was beaten by the pounding waves and flooded with sea water.

Most of *Tiger*'s cargo was lost or ruined before she could be beached and repaired sufficiently to set sail again. The *Tiger* journal, obviously written by someone not favorably disposed toward Ferdinando, gave the story in a single concise sentence: "The 29. wee waighed anker to bring the Tyger into the harbour, where through the unskilfulnesse of the Master whose name was Fernando, the Admirall strooke on grounde, and sunke."

Certainly this was not an auspicious beginning for

Grenville's attempt to plant England's first permanent colony in what is now the United States of America, but even as the sunken *Tiger* was being salvaged, good news was received from a nearby Outer Banks island. Some thirty Englishmen had been discovered on Croatoan, near Cape Hatteras, left there three weeks earlier by Captain George Raymond of *Lion*. The supposition is that, finding none of the other vessels of Grenville's fleet at the Outer Banks rendezvous, and no doubt fretting for action and adventure, Raymond had decided to sail on up the coast toward Newfoundland, but had left a small detachment at Cape Hatteras, probably with the intention of returning later to pick them up if Grenville had not arrived by then. As for the other ships that had been scattered in the Bay of Portugal storm, there are later indications that *Roebuck*, and possibly *Dorothy* and the second pinnace, eventually rejoined the admiral.

The time had come to explore the surrounding area, to try to verify the stories Amadas and Barlowe had heard the previous year of Secotan and of the land of the Neuse, for summer was well advanced and Grenville had yet to select a site for his settlement. Here, in the *Tiger* journal entry for July 6, 1585, is the first mention in almost a year of either of the two Indians, Manteo and Wanchese, who had returned to England with Amadas and Barlowe. When Grenville sent a small detachment to the mainland as a sort of advance party, Manteo served as guide. They returned with a favorable report, and Grenville made ready to cross the sounds and see for himself what the territory was really like.

The expedition was planned carefully; some fifty men traveled in four shallow-draft boats, fully equipped with food and supplies for at least eight days. Grenville led the procession, riding in style with several of his gentlemen advisers in the bow of his tilt boat, an awning protecting them from the sun. The main force rode in the new pinnace that had been built at Muskito Bay, with Thomas

Cavendish and Ralph Lane aboard. Cavendish was probably master of the ship and Lane, commander of the troops. Ten more men, under captains Amadas and Clarke, were on board a ship's boat, with John White and others, also in a ship's boat, bringing up the rear.

In less than a week the little flotilla covered a lot of territory, traveling as far north as "the great lake called by the Savages Paquype" (modern Lake Mattamuskeet), and as far south as the mouth of the Neuse River and Core Sound. They visited three Indian villages—Secotan, Pomeiooc, and Aquascogoc—apparently establishing a basis for friendly relations with the natives at each stop.

But before returning to the fleet at Wococon, Grenville reverted to the high-handed ways he had demonstrated in his dealings with the Spaniards on Puerto Rico. "One of our boates with the Admirall was sent to Aquascococke to demaund a silver cup which one of the Savages had stolen from us, and not receiving it according to his promise, we burnt, and spoyled their corne, and Towne, all the people beeing fledde." Grenville, obviously a man of fire and flame, was no doubt pleased with this demonstration to the savages that they could not trifle with those who had come from Europe to share their land. But others were to rue the day Aquascogoc was set to the torch.

The official journal provides no more information on this memorable expedition, this first effort of the English to explore the interior lands beyond the Carolina sounds, so it is necessary once more to turn to the artist White for missing details. He must have been exceptionally busy with his brush and watercolors during those relatively brief stops at the Indian villages, for though there is no indication of his having visited the area later, his Carolina drawings include illuminating views of two of the Indian towns, Pomeiooc and Secotan.

The Pomeiooc drawing shows a small Indian village surrounded by a circular stockade of high poles. The largest of the eighteen structures within the stockade is the temple, described as "builded rownde, and covered with skynne matts." All of the remaining structures are rectangular in shape, some with open ends and sides to let in the air, and others with woven mats covering the openings. With their rounded roofs many of them have the shape and appearance of an ordinary loaf of bread.

The Secotan drawing is considerably more revealing, although White chose to show only a representative part of what was described as the main town of Wingina's far-flung empire. Connected by carefully manicured streets and paths, the buildings are for the most part of the same design as those in Pomeiooc—rectangular in shape, with rounded roofs. Off to one side are three fields of corn, representing the crop in various stages of growth—the first one, "corne newly sprong"; the second, "their greene corne"; and the third, "their rype corne." A large building is described as the "tombe" for their dead; a lake in the background is identified as "from whence they fetche their water." Some Indians are depicted hunting deer in a nearby wood. Several others are shown seated at a meal, with still others dancing in a circle in performance of a religious rite.

White also prepared detailed maps, which provide a general understanding of the location of the Indian villages visited by Grenville's party. Pomeiooc was situated just east of the northern end of Lake Mattamuskeet, between the twentieth-century communities of Englehard and New Holland. Aquascogoc, the village set to the torch by Grenville, was a short distance southwest of Mattamuskeet, probably between Belhaven and Pantego. Secotan was on the south side of the Pamlico River, downstream from Chocowinity. Recent efforts by archaeologists to locate these three sites have been fruitless, partly because of the existence of numerous other Indian sites in the same general area and partly, in the case of Secotan at least, for want of more precise information as to the location.

If one of Grenville's reasons for stopping at Wococon and exploring the surrounding territory was to search for an alternate site for establishing the colony, then he must have changed his mind. The near loss of his flagship on the inlet bar was reason enough for concern, and that incident probably convinced him that reliance on such a harbor would make settlement in that region impractical.

Even before his visit to the mainland villages, Grenville had sent word of his arrival to King Wingina on Roanoke Island, and July 21 the fleet weighed anchor and sailed north from Wococon. They must have run into bad weather, for if the *Tiger* journal is to be used as a guide to the chronology of the expedition, it took them almost a week to sail the relatively short distance—less than a hundred miles—to Port Ferdinando. Two days after their arrival on July 29, Granganimeo, "brother to King Wingino, came aboord the Admirall, and Manteo with him."

Raleigh's would-be colonists had finally reached their new home in America. The passage from England to the Outer Banks of North Carolina had produced one crisis after another—a tempest at sea off Portugal; encounters with the Spaniards on Puerto Rico; shipwreck at Wococon Inlet; and confrontation with the Indians at Aquascogoc over a missing silver cup. The real danger to the success of the venture, however, was much more subtle, for even before the arrival at Port Ferdinando an undercurrent of dissension among the expedition's officers and gentlemen had threatened to erupt into open conflict.

The primary antagonists were Grenville and Lane, top men in the chain of command. A keen observer might have sensed trouble between the two early on, and certainly by the time they were ready to depart Muskito Bay. Lane, the veteran soldier with direct access to Secretary of State Walsingham and others of influence, was an enthusiastic supporter of the plan advanced by Sir Francis Drake and Sir Philip Sidney to establish English bases in the West Indies from which to carry out raids against the

FIGURE 4. *The town of Pomeiooc. Engraving by Theodor de Bry from a drawing by John White.*

FIGURE 5. *The town of Secotan. Engraving by Theodor de Bry from a drawing by John White.*

Spaniards. He could well have had Drake's plan in mind when he produced what would appear to be excessively formidable defensive works at Muskito Bay. If so, he would not have taken kindly to Grenville's order to destroy the facilities as soon as the pinnace was launched.

The conflict was brought into the open shortly thereafter as a result of Grenville's decision to send Lane off to Cape Rojo for salt, with assurances that there were no Spaniards in the area to offer resistance. In an open council meeting following his return Lane complained bitterly that he had been misled; that he should never have been sent on such a mission with a force of only twenty-five men, and half a dozen Spanish prisoners armed with "mattockes and spades"; and that their lives and the success of the whole effort had been seriously jeopardized when he was confronted by what he described as a Spanish force of forty horsemen and three hundred foot soldiers under an experienced commander.

Thereafter, those council meetings, with the key officers and gentlemen sitting in, must have been something to observe. Lane contended in a later letter to Walsingham that Grenville had threatened to put him on trial for his life because in one such meeting he offered advice that did not jibe with what the general had in mind.

But Lane and Grenville were not the only ones involved. Simon Ferdinando was having his own troubles with the general, especially when Grenville—or whoever was keeping the *Tiger* journal for him—blamed the pilot, in the strongest of language, for the stranding of the flagship at Wococon. Others siding with Lane against Grenville included Thomas Cavendish, the expedition's high marshal; Francis Brooke, the treasurer; and Captain John Clarke of *Roebuck*. Historian Quinn thinks the threat against Lane might have been "only an instance of Grenville's hot temper," but adds that it is not at all unlikely the other problems may have come about because Grenville assumed "too many of the prerogatives of justice to please Cavendish as high marshal."

Whether or not Grenville, as Lane claimed, "demeaned himselfe" from the day he took command at Plymouth until his departure from Port Ferdinando and conducted himself in a tyrannical manner throughout, only those participating in the venture could have known. But Lane did make clear to Walsingham that he wanted never again to be placed in the position of having to serve under or with Sir Richard Grenville.

Unfortunately, there is no information available on how these two antagonists conducted themselves during the three-week period in August, 1585, between their arrival at Port Ferdinando and Grenville's departure for England, for there could be no more critical time in the history of Raleigh's colonization efforts. Certainly both Grenville and Lane had to visit the village of Wingina and Granganimeo on the north end of Roanoke Island and agree on a site nearby for the first English settlement. Innumerable other decisions of importance faced Lane, who was to remain on Roanoke Island as commander of the settlement, and Grenville, who had overall responsibility. What type of fortifications would be necessary? Would the dwellings and other buildings be constructed within the fort, or nearby? Should some sort of defensive works be built at Port Ferdinando to ward off possible Spanish attacks? How much of this work would be completed before Grenville's departure? How many men would be left with Lane to establish the colony?

One decision was made early. Just a few days after contact had been made with the Indians on Roanoke Island and Granganimeo had visited the vessels riding at anchor in Port Ferdinando, a small expeditionary force under Captain Amadas was dispatched to Weapemeoc, which was the Indian name for Albemarle Sound and the adjacent land area. Amadas probably went as far west as the Chowan and Roanoke rivers and visited several villages on the north side of the sound, including Pasquenoke, "the womans Towne."

It had been nearly four months since the departure of

Grenville's fleet from Plymouth, and the time had come to send a messenger back home to report to Raleigh and his fellow backers on their safe arrival in Virginia and their decision to establish the first settlement on Roanoke Island. Grenville chose John Arundell for this assignment, and he departed the Outer Banks on August 5 in one of the smaller vessels.

Grenville's plan, apparently, was to begin his own voyage home in *Tiger* a week later, for under date of August 12 Lane wrote several confidential letters, including two to Walsingham and one to Sidney. Grenville did not actually depart, however, until August 25, leaving at least one other vessel behind to make the journey later. By that time it is almost certain that Lane's Roanoke Island fort had been completed and that enough other structures had been built to protect the men and their supplies from the elements.

No contemporary drawing exists of Lane's fort, nor is there any written description. Known today as Fort Raleigh, a national historic site administered by the National Park Service, it has been the scene of sufficient archaeological excavation to determine its size and shape. The Fort Raleigh earthworks, as reconstructed under the direction of Park Service archaeologist J. C. Harrington, are quite similar to those erected by Lane at the Puerto Rico salt works. The two fortifications are of approximately the same size, measuring some seventy feet across, and are basically square, with appendages on the side in which guns could have been mounted or musketeers could have taken up their positions. Quinn describes the final product as "a modified star-shaped fort, based on a square laid out on the ground and embellished with bastions."

In one of his accounts, Lane mentioned the existence of a structure, or structures, within the line of earthworks. The archaeologists found sufficient evidence to conclude that this consisted either of a single building approxi-

FIGURE 6. *John White drawing of Ralph Lane's fortifications at the Cape Rojo salt works (© 1964 The Trustees of the British Museum; print courtesy of the North Carolina Collection, University of North Carolina at Chapel Hill).*

mately ten feet wide and thirty-five feet long or two separate buildings occupying the same space. Later references to a lower floor indicate that there was a second story.

It seems obvious that the colonists did not live inside this fortification but constructed dwellings and other buildings nearby. Cursory attempts to locate this "cittie of Ralegh," the first English town in America, have produced no reliable leads. Harrington and Quinn seem to feel that it was located north or west of the fort, in the general direction of Wingina's Indian town, but close enough to Fort Raleigh that the occupants could seek shelter and protection there in a short time if threatened by attack either from their native neighbors or the Spaniards.

The fort was constructed some distance back from the edge of the body of water east of Roanoke Island, and it can be assumed that a sufficient area between the fort and the sound was cleared of forest growth to enable the defenders to command the approach from the water side with at least one mounted gun. This would have provided those within the fort with an unobstructed view of what is now Roanoke Sound and, beyond it, the sand hills at Nags Head on the Outer Banks. Hints that there was a protected cove below the fort, with sufficient water depth to accommodate a small pinnace, cannot be substantiated for there has been considerable change in the shoreline on the north end of the island. In recent times, in fact, the sand bottom has shelved off so gradually near the fort that a person can wade out hundreds of yards before encountering water deep enough to float anything larger than a canoe or skiff.

It is likely that the majority of Grenville's soldiers were pressed into service to complete the earthworks at the fort and to transport supplies and equipment from the harbor to Roanoke Island before Grenville departed. He had at his disposal at least 300 of these armed men, all of whom were potential members of the first colony, yet left only 107 of them—or 108, depending on whose word you take—when he returned to England. The only plausible explanation advanced for his taking nearly 200 prospective colonists back home with him was that the loss of *Tiger*'s cargo at Wococon had so depleted the supplies that there was concern for the survival of a full complement of men on Roanoke Island. Or, again, the dissension between Grenville and Lane may have been a factor.

Grenville set sail for England on August 25, 1585. Six days later, on the high seas, *Tiger* encountered a three-hundred-ton Spanish ship laden with a rich cargo. The *Tiger* journal notes only that the Spanish merchantman was taken as a prize, though there is an unusual reference to Grenville's boarding her "with a boate made with boards of chests, which fell a sunder, and sunke at the shippes side, assoone as ever hee and his men were out of it." If this meant that Grenville had undertaken the ocean passage without a tender or some other sort of small boat aboard, then he was an even less experienced commander than has been pictured.

Grenville was aboard the captured Spanish vessel, rather than his flagship, when bad weather was encountered ten days later and the two vessels were separated. *Tiger*, apparently with Simon Ferdinando at the helm, reached the coast of England on October 6, and anchored at Falmouth the same day. Grenville, in his Spanish prize, did not arrive for another twelve days, but was "courteously received by diverse of his worshipfull friends." Whether, en route, he had surreptitiously opened and read the letters he was carrying from Lane to Walsingham and Sidney is a matter for speculation, but there is no indication that the two men to whom Raleigh had entrusted this venture, Ralph Lane and Sir Richard Grenville, ever again had personal contact.

Following Grenville's departure, as the men grew accustomed to life at their Roanoke Island base, Lane took time to prepare additional reports, including a letter to Richard Hakluyt, the elder, dated September 3 and another one to

Walsingham dated September 8. It is assumed that these letters were sent back to England on the last ship to leave America, probably Clarke's flyboat, *Roebuck*.

Lane's letter to Walsingham was primarily a defense of his own actions in the dispute with Grenville and of the conduct of Cavendish, Brooke, Clarke, and others who had run afoul of the general. He also provided one bit of new information, this dealing with the extent of the native population in the surrounding area. The area to the west of Roanoke Island, he said, was so heavily peopled that the Indian towns were located at three-mile intervals. He also claimed that members of his company had visited and witnessed a green corn festival for which "aboove 700 personnes, yonge and olde together," had gathered.

Lane's other letter, the one to the elder Hakluyt, read like a publicist's promotional piece, describing discoveries made on the mainland in the brief period following Grenville's departure. He began by referring to the mainland area as "the goodliest soile under the cope of heaven" in which the natural products of the fields and forests, which surpassed in value even those of Spain, France, and Italy, were just waiting to be plucked and savored by Elizabeth's subjects. The climate, he continued, was "so wholesome, that we have not had one sicke, since we touched land here," and the native Americans were "most curteous" and very desirous of acquiring English clothes, especially items made of coarse cloth rather than silk. As Barlowe had reported a year earlier, the Indians were willing to pay a premium price in barter for copper. Lane dated his letter "from the new Fort in Virginia, this 3. September, 1585."

With the departure of the last of the vessels of the fleet, Lane and his 106 fellow colonists were alone on the North American mainland, surrounded by Indians, wary of possible attack by Spaniards, yet very likely excited at being the first Englishmen to take up residence on this "goodliest soile under the cope of heaven."

CHAPTER 8

The Native Americans

All of the numerous voyages to America by Englishmen during the three-quarters of a century following John Cabot's 1497 expedition to Newfoundland were but prelude to the establishment of the first English settlement in America, on Roanoke Island, in 1585.

This was the beginning of residency by Englishmen in what was to become the United States, the first time that subjects of the British crown lived for an extended period on the North American mainland. Yet few Americans have ever heard of the Ralph Lane settlement, for it is seldom mentioned in texts used in the study and teaching of American history.

The documentation is readily available and, with one exception, has been available for nearly four hundred years. It is found in five different sources, which frequently corroborate or expand on each other: (1) the accounts of Grenville's 1585 voyage to Roanoke Island with Lane and his colonists; (2) an extensive report on the settlement, written by Lane, its governor; (3) the drawings John White made during his stay of approximately one year in Virginia, long thought to have been lost, but later rediscovered; (4) Thomas Hariot's *Briefe and True Report of the New Found Land of Virginia*, a fascinating book first published in 1588; and (5) Theodor de Bry's engravings for the 1590 edition of Hariot's *Briefe and True*

FIGURE 7. *Title page from Thomas Hariot's* Briefe and True Report of the New Found Land of Virginia.

Report, which were based on White's drawings. All of these except White's drawings and de Bry's engravings have been printed in various editions of Hakluyt's *Principall Navigations*.

It was not by chance that the complement of England's first American colony included two such highly qualified specialists as White the artist and Hariot the scientist, for Raleigh had planned it so. And he must have been pleased with the result, for there emerged from this joint effort the first clear picture of the native American Indians. From it we know not only of their appearance but of how they lived and worshiped, and the way they harvested their crops, and built their boats, and fished, and hunted, and warred.

Thomas Hariot (the tendency now is to spell the name "Harriot," though it appears with only one *r* on the title page of his most famous work) was the younger member of the team, twenty-five-years old in 1585, and already an important figure in Raleigh's household, where he served as a tutor in science and mathematics. Paul Hulton, a leading authority on White's drawings and Hariot's *Briefe and True Report*, is of the opinion that Hariot's scientific knowledge, and especially his understanding of navigation, probably "acted as a stimulus to Raleigh's concern with overseas exploration." Hariot is known to have provided navigational instructions for Amadas and Barlowe, to have made astronomical observations on the 1585 voyage, and to have kept extensive scientific records of what he saw in America. In addition, he has since been recognized as the founder of the English school of algebra, as the designer and builder of one of the earliest telescopes, and as the discoverer of the law of refraction, or bending of light.

Hariot's greatest contribution to Raleigh's colonization efforts, however, may have been in an entirely different field—that of linguistics. He was possibly the first Englishman to learn to speak and understand the language of the native residents of North America. Modern historians speculate that Manteo and Wanchese, the two Indians who returned to England with Amadas and Barlowe in the fall of 1584 and spent the winter there, were housed at Raleigh's estate, and that Hariot was assigned the task of learning to converse with them. Besides teaching them basic English, this would have involved his acquiring a working knowledge of their native tongue. Thus, when Hariot finally arrived on Roanoke Island in the summer of 1585, he could well have been prepared, as no other Englishman had been before him, to gain a full understanding of what Indian life was really like.

For all of his diverse talents, Hariot might best have been a clergyman, for throughout his writings he places emphasis on the religious beliefs of the Indians and on his own efforts to convert them to Christianity. "Manie times and in every towne where I came," he wrote, "I made declaration of the contentes of the Bible; that therein was set foorth the true and onelie GOD, and his mightie woorkes" and the "true doctrine of salvation through Christ." Ironically, he was later to be labeled an atheist, but on Roanoke Island he seemed almost obsessed with spreading the gospel.

Hariot soon learned, and in fact probably had already learned from Manteo and Wanchese in England, that the Indians had a religion of their own, one in which some beliefs were not too different from those of Protestants. "Although it be farre from the truth," Hariot said of the Algonkian religion, "there is hope it may bee the easier and sooner reformed."

The foundation of the Indian religion was that there was "one onely chiefe and great God, which hath bene from all eternitie." When this chief and great God decided to create the world, he found it necessary to make petty gods, one in the form of the sun, another the moon, and still others the stars. He created the water next, then delegated to the lesser gods the task of creating the great "diversitie of creatures" that were to inhabit the earth. As for mankind: "They say a woman was made first, which by the working of one of the goddes, conceived and brought foorth children."

The Indians represented all of their gods "by images in the formes of men, which they call Kewasowak," with a single such idol called a Kewas. Hariot said the Kewasowak were housed in special buildings, or temples, where the Indians worshiped, sang, and made "manie times offering unto them." Some of the temples housed only a single Kewas, while others had two or three. White pictured one Kewas, a life-sized figure, fully clothed, and wearing a broad-brimmed conical hat, sitting on a platform in a burial tomb and guarding the mummified remains of deceased chieftains. One of the larger temples, shown in an engraving of the White drawing of the town of Pomeiooc, was a circular structure with a pagodalike roof covered with mats made of animal skins.

According to Hariot's report the Indians had their own heaven and hell, and believed strongly in "the immortalitie of the soule." Following death, and "as soone as the soule is departed from the bodie," he said, it is carried either to heaven "the habitacle of the gods, there to enjoy perpetuall blisse and happinesse" or to "a great pitte or hole," located in the furthest part of the world toward the sun, "there to burne continually." Their name for this place of perpetual residence for the wicked was Popogusso, and in life they tried their best to conduct themselves in a manner that would preclude the possibility of ending up there.

The Indian sought guidance and protection from his gods in almost every conceivable circumstance, from birth to death, and even after. He prayed, danced, and shook his rattles in an effort to pacify his gods before going into battle, during battle, and even after the battle was over. He sought godly sanction when going hunting or fishing, or just out for a ride in his canoe; and he invariably turned to prayer when threatened by storm or devastated by drought and when ill, injured, or just feeble from the infirmities of age. He was in truth, by his own precepts, a devout disciple of his gods.

The appearance of the strangely garbed, white-skinned men in their huge winged craft, the sound and devastation wrought by their weapons, and numerous evidences of their seemingly mystical powers caused some to think that these beings might themselves be gods, direct representatives of their own great and only Kewas, the biblical father of Christ. Hariot was to learn later just how much bearing these thoughts would have on his own missionary work.

It was common practice for the Indians to accompany their prayers by offering sacrifices to their gods, and they carried with them for this purpose on all of their travels and adventures small pouches filled with the crushed and powdered dry leaves of a plant they called uppowoc. Hariot said uppowoc was held in such "precious estimation amongest them," that they thought their gods were "marvelously delighted therwith" and so offered it to them often. During religious ceremonies they would build large fires, paying special tribute to the gods by casting uppowoc on the flames. Whenever a new fishing weir was set they scattered the powdered leaves about to bring good luck. And only a foolhardy Indian would have considered venturing very far from shore in his canoe without carrying with him a packet of uppowoc, to be cast into the air and spread upon the waters when a storm arose. Hariot said the offering was often accompanied by unusual gestures, stamping, dancing and clapping. Those caught up in the religious fervor, he added, would hold up their hands and stare into the heavens, all the while "chattering strange words & noises."

They grew uppowoc in carefully tended plots near their houses and dried it in a time-consuming curing process, before cutting or crushing it into smaller particles. The

Indians had yet another use for the cured uppowoc: as described by Hariot, they "take the fume or smoke thereof by sucking it thorough pipes made of claie, into their stomacke and heade: from whence it purgeth superfluous fleame & other grosse humours, openeth all the pores & passages of the body." This marvelous substance, medicine both to the body and to the soul, was grown also in certain parts of the West Indies, according to Hariot, with "divers names," though "The Spaniardes generally call it Tobacco."

The Algonkian Indians living in the Roanoke Island area grew other crops in addition to uppowoc, for they were, basically, an agricultural people. Maize, or corn, was a staple of their diet and the one crop without which they would have had difficulty surviving. Hariot said some of the Indian farmers "have two harvests, as we have heard, out of one and the same ground." This statement was probably closer to the truth than Barlowe's report, a year earlier, that the corn "groweth three times in five moneths: in Maye they sowe, in July they reape, in June they sowe, in August they reape: in July they sowe, in September they reape," though in his Secotan drawing White shows corn in three stages of growth.

Hariot left a detailed description of how the Indians planted, tended, and harvested their corn. "The ground they never fatten with mucke, dounge, or any other thing," he said, nor do they "plow nor digge it as we in England." Instead, a few days before the time for sowing, the men and women would take to the fields together, breaking only enough of the surface soil to remove weeds, grass, and old corn stubs. The men, walking between the rows, used hoelike wooden instruments with long handles. The women, accustomed to working while squatting or sitting, used much shorter tools, which Hariot described as "peckers or parers." As soon as the weeds and stubble had dried for a few days, all of the material was scraped up into small piles and burned. "And this," Hariot added, "is all the husbanding of their ground that they use."

When the time came for planting, Hariot continued, "beginning in one corner of the plot, with a pecker they make a hole, wherein they put foure grains." It was a meticulous operation: they carefully spaced the grains of seed corn about an inch apart before covering them with rich earth, or "moulde," to form small hills. Then they left approximately a yard of open ground between the hills, "where according to discretion here and there" they planted as many beans and peas as would grow without affecting or being affected by the taller corn. The Indians also grew a variety of roots, including potatoes, as well as melons, gourds, and several different vegetables in or near the cornfields. Even small plots of pumpkins and sunflowers are shown in the Secotan drawing.

In addition to harvesting these special crops the Algonkians took advantage of the natural bounties of the forests, picking wild fruit, berries, and nuts in season. They relied heavily on the meat of wild animals and fowl and on fish for their food, and the Indian men spent much of their time hunting and fishing, combining sport with the quest for food. Lacking conventional tools, they employed a high degree of ingenuity in devising methods for catching or killing fish and game.

The Europeans were especially impressed with their fishing techniques, which proved much more effective in the shallow sounds surrounding Roanoke Island than those employed by the colonists. For the most part the Indians caught their fish in netlike obstructions called weirs, which they placed across streams or channels, much as modern pound-netters do to catch the seasonal runs of striped bass and shad. The weirs were made of reeds, woven or tied together and anchored to the bottom by poles stuck into the sand. With their tops extending above the surface of the water the weirs looked much like fences. They were arranged in varied patterns designed to catch the fish and then impound them.

Hariot added that yet another fishing technique "which is more strange, is with poles made sharpe at one ende, by shooting them into the fish after the maner as Irishmen cast dartes." The spears or harpoons used in this operation were fitted with sharp points, some of them made from the hollow tail of what Hariot described as "a certaine fishe like to a sea crabbe." The Indians were adept at spearing fish, whether wading in shallow waters or fishing from their canoes, and apparently they fished at night as well as in the daytime, probably using torches of lightwood knots both for illumination and as a means of attracting fish to the surface.

The Englishmen reported that the Indians caught a wide variety of fish, ranging from trout, mullet, and flounder to giant rays and porpoise. Hariot added that there were "many other sortes of excellent good fish, which we have taken & eaten, whose names I know not but in the countrey language," some of which are pictured by White in his watercolors. In the months of February, March, April, and May, Hariot added, there were large quantities of sturgeon and herring, some of the latter ranging up to "two foote in length and better."

As was the case with most other American Indians, the natives of the Albemarle and Pamlico Sound regions relied to a great degree on bows and arrows for hunting. Hariot made special mention of black bears, which he said were "good meat," and he described how the Indians would chase the bears until they sought safety by climbing a tree, "whence with arrowes they are shot downe starke dead." Hunting the fleet-footed deer with bow and arrow called for different skills, but the Indians had devised a special technique there as well, and one involving a high degree of cunning and patience. After foraging for food, the deer would often seek protection in areas covered by high reeds and underbrush, where they could sleep in relative security. But the crafty Indians, having observed the habits of the deer, would hide in the reeds for hours, waiting for their quarry to return so they could shoot them at close range.

The wide assortment of food items available to the Indians called for varied methods of preparation and preservation. Most of the fruit and nuts and some of the vegetables were eaten raw, but the meat and fish and other foods had to be cooked before being consumed. They did their cooking outside over open fires, since they had no flues or chimneys in their houses. Most of the cooking was done in handmade, round-bottomed earthen pots resting on small mounds of dirt, with carefully tended fires underneath. In this way they boiled or stewed a wide variety of native foods including meat, fish, fruit, nuts, roots, and such vegetables as corn, potatoes, beans, and peas. They also broiled certain items, including fish and meat. In one of his drawings White pictures fish laid out on an elevated grill made of reeds, the grill in turn supported and kept away from the flame by four large stakes driven into the ground. Dried and smoked meat and fish were preserved along with corn and certain roots and nuts for use during the winter season. In the spring, when the reserve supply had been depleted, they went over to the seashore "to live upon shell fishe" while "their grownds be in sowing, and their corne growing." In the process they accumulated vast mounds of shells at their favorite meeting places.

They seem to have had a wider variety of bread than the average modern American family. Usually they made their bread from corn or wheatlike grain, but sometimes, for variety, they boiled beans or peas, mashed them in a mortar, and shaped them into "loaves or lumps of dowishe bread." They did the same with walnuts and chestnuts, pounding the meat into a great mushy meal which they served as a sort of spoonbread. They even made bread of acorns, first drying them "upon hurdles made of reeds with fire underneath," then storing the cooked nuts until they were needed, at which time they soaked them in water and mashed them into a kind of dough.

The dishes used by the Indians were described by Barlowe as "woodden platters of sweete timber"; and wood was undoubtedly the material from which they made their ladles and spoons. Gourds, which they cultivated in their fields, served as containers for liquids.

At mealtime, instead of sitting around tables, the Indians sat on large stitched or woven mats of reeds, which were spread on the ground. The men and women customarily sat facing each other with the food in large wooden plates or bowls between them, and they picked up food with their fingers. For the most part the Indians appear to have been very careful not to overeat, leading one of the colonists to describe them as "verye sober in their eatinge, and drinkinge, and consequentlye verye longe lived because they doe not oppress nature."

The Indian houses were made of "small poles made fast at the tops in rounde forme after the maner as is used in many arbories in our gardens of England." Normally rectangular in shape, with their length "commonly double to the breadth" and ranging from thirty-six to more than seventy feet long, the houses were usually covered with bark, although Hariot said he saw some covered with "artificiall mattes made of long rushes, from the tops of the houses downe to the ground."

Despite their lack of tools the native Americans were expert boat builders, and both Barlowe and Hariot described their unusual technique in detail. Selecting "some great tree," preferably one that had been blown down in a storm, they began by burning through the massive trunk to get the approximate length desired. After scraping off the bark with sharp shells, they began the laborious process of burning out the interior. This was accomplished by spreading gum or rosin "upon one side thereof," then cutting away the coals with shells. They repeated the process

FIGURE 8. Their manner of fishynge in Virginia. *Engraving by Theodor de Bry from a drawing by John White.*

FIGURE 9. *Cooking in earthen pots. Engraving by Theodor de Bry from a drawing by John White.*

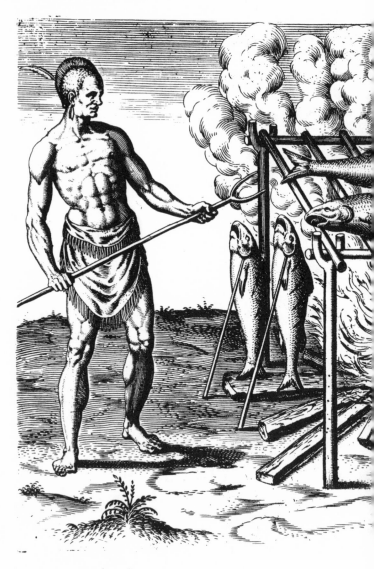

FIGURE 10. *Broiling fish. Engraving by Theodor de Bry from a drawing by John White.*

.J 4.

FIGURE II. Their sitting at meate. *Engraving by Theodor de Bry from a drawing by John White.*

FIGURE 12. The manner of makinge their boates. *Engraving by Theodor de Bry from a drawing by John White.*

time after time, first spreading and setting fire to the gum, then chipping away with the shells, until the craft finally took shape. "In this way," Barlowe said, "they fashion very fine boats and such as will transport twenty men."

The English chroniclers have left us with considerable detailed information on the appearance of the natives, and especially on the way they dressed. Most clothes were made of deerskin. The women pictured in White's drawings wore apronlike skirts extending from their waists downward to above their knees, with their breasts exposed. Some of the men wore similar skirts, while others were dressed in full-length capes, either draped over the left shoulder or tied behind the neck. Most often the material was slit to form tassels, and when attending "solemne feasts" or preparing for hunting expeditions the men would sometimes attach long tails to the rears of their garments.

The conjurers, or medicine men, would "fasten a small black birde above one of their ears as a badge of their office" and carry a bag attached to a belt or rope around their waists. The priests, on the other hand, wore "a shorte clocke made of fine hares skinnes quilted with the hayre outwarde" and were further identified by having "their heare cutt like a creste, on the topps of thier heades as other doe, but the rest are cutt shorte, savinge those which growe above their foreheads in manner of a perriwigge." All of the women shown in the drawings had their hair trimmed in bangs; most wore their hair shortly cropped on the sides, while others had longer hair hanging down in the rear or tied in a loose knot.

The Indians used cosmetics extensively, on their bodies as well as their faces, and often had permanent body markings. In most instances the women decorated their arms with either body paint or tattoos in fairly intricate designs that made them appear almost as though they were wearing armlets. Some had similar designs on their legs and equally elaborate facial makeup. Such decorations did not usually appear on the men. When visiting other villages, engaging in religious ceremonies or festivities, or preparing for battle, however, they painted their backs with distinctive symbols to identify their tribe and the individual's status within the tribe.

Although several of the women pictured wore necklaces, the men usually outdid them, with ornaments in their ears in addition to those around their necks. Wingina and the other "cheiff Lordes" wore chains of copper "beades" or "smoothe bone" about their necks. Others strung pearls from their ears and wore bracelets of pearls on their arms "in token of authoritye, and honor."

From these verbal descriptions by Hariot and his associates, supplemented with the detailed drawings of White, there begins to emerge a coherent picture of the life-style of the native people. They lived in neatly organized villages, sometimes in houses with several rooms. They maintained orderly and productive fields; worshiped their gods; hunted and fished when they needed to, or when the urge was overwhelming; and adhered to common sense and their own established rules of etiquette when dining. There were wars, of course, and periods of drought; and on occasion devastating hurricanes moved up from the Caribbean. But in many respects it was a nearly idyllic existence. Until, that is, the civilized Englishmen arrived.

CHAPTER 9

The First Winter in America

A detachment of 107 men was left behind at Ralph Lane's new fort on Roanoke Island when the last vessel of Grenville's patched-up fleet weighed anchor off the Outer Banks and began the long voyage home to England in the early fall of 1585. This was far short of the 800 men originally recommended, or even of the approximately 300 available to Grenville, and it constituted an inadequate force with which to colonize a continent.

Grenville promised Lane that he would be back the following spring—by Easter, according to Lane's understanding—with vessels laden with supplies, equipment, and reinforcements. During the intervening seven months, from early autumn through winter and into the following spring, this pitifully small garrison was to be pretty much on its own, short of food, living in an alien land, surrounded by "savage heathens." Nonetheless, they were expected to make a concerted effort to explore the surrounding territory, especially to the west and north, not only to get the lay of the land but to look for gold and copper and other metals and, if possible, to locate other, more advantageous sites for future settlement.

Lane was in complete command, the governor of "Virginia," an area extending from Spanish Florida in the south to the New England coast (Norumbega) to the north and the Pacific to the west—in short, most of what would later become the United States. Philip Amadas appears to have been the number-two man, officially listed as "Admirall of the countrie." But Amadas was an admiral in name only, for he had at his disposal only a motley collection of small craft suitable for use in the shallow interior waters surrounding Roanoke Island—the Muskito Bay pinnace; a couple of four-oar wherries, sometimes referred to as double wherries, each of which was large enough to carry about fifteen men and their equipment; plus an assemblage of small boats.

In the military chain of command, Master Edward Stafford headed up Lane's first company, with a second one apparently under Captain John Vaughan. Master Thomas Harvie, a one-time London grocer, was the "Cape Merchant" of the colony, charged with responsibility for keeping track of all supplies, dispensing food and equipment as needed, and supervising the bartering activities with the natives. Thomas Hariot was the scientist, historian, and interpreter; John White, the artist and surveyor.

Of the 107 men the names of 14 were listed with the prefix "master," including Amadas, Stafford, Harvie, and Hariot, indicating that these were the gentlemen of the colony, the leaders and possibly in some instances investors in the venture, and thus the nucleus of Lane's governing council. Of the remaining colonists it appears that some were Irishmen, including an Edward Nugent, who was identified as Lane's personal servant. There were several Welshmen and Germans, a Dutchman, and even a Czech Jew, in addition to native Englishmen drawn from different parts of the mother country. Some may have been miners, but there is no indication that the group included all the various artisans and craftsmen considered so essential by Hakluyt.

It would be helpful if we had available a full chronology of that winter of 1585–86 when England's first American colonists settled in for their stay on Roanoke Island. Hariot indicates that he prepared such a diarylike record, and Lane may have also, but many such papers and some of White's drawings were lost at sea the following summer. What we do have, therefore, is a considerable amount of information about events during that winter but no dates with which to pin them down, though there is enough specific data to piece together a rough chronology for the spring months.

The brief exploratory expedition by Amadas to the westward through the Albemarle Sound area had produced enough information to whet Lane's appetite for a closer look himself, but other matters had to be attended to first in and around the fort and settlement. There was, at the outset, the matter of securing food for the winter, and this involved the establishment of a close relationship with Wingina and his people. As a result of these efforts the Indians provided fresh fish from their weirs and corn from their reserve supply, though it is difficult to determine how much of this was arranged through barter and how much resulted from persuasion, fear, and force.

It is easy, however, to picture the inquisitive Hariot, in conversation with Manteo, Wanchese, and others of the natives, getting bits and pieces of information on native plants and how they were grown and used; on Indian life and beliefs; on religion, and warfare, and tradition. At Lane's urging he must have also spent considerable time pressing his native friends for details about the territories controlled by other chieftains and about relationships, friendly or warlike, between the different villages and tribes. The preparation of maps was of the utmost importance, and here it can be assumed that Hariot and White worked as a team with the artist preparing rough preliminary sketch maps based partly on personal observation and partly on information gained from the natives by Hariot. Apparently, White had already sent back to England with one of the returning vessels a number of the drawings he had made at Secotan and Pomeiooc and on Roanoke Island.

By the time Grenville departed, it was much too late in the season for the Englishmen to plant any crops, and Lane, the soldier, seemed little interested in having his men study the Indian ways in order to become adept at the highly successful native fishing methods. As they gathered more and more information, they received hints of treasures of another sort to be found beyond Wingina's realm: of pearl fisheries in a great inland sea to the north and of mountains of gold to the west. Since Grenville had already explored the territory to the south—Secotan, Aquascogoc, and Pomeiooc and the lake known as Paquippe—Lane made only a cursory effort to learn more of that area, sending the pinnace on a short outing into Pamlico Sound, and complained later that the water was too shallow to accommodate the vessel.

The rumors of pearls to the north seemed to hold more promise. Early in the winter Lane dispatched an expedition in that direction, probably under Amadas, which explored as far north as the tributaries of Chesapeake Bay, the land of the Chesepians. Apparently a small base was established in the Chesapeake Bay area, and some who have studied the meager records of that winter are convinced that a detachment of Lane's men spent several months in the vicinity of the Chesepian town of Skicoak. But if they did, there is no hard evidence as to exactly who or how many they were, or of what they did or what they may have learned. The only pearls the colonists mentioned were black ones, of little value, and even these probably were acquired through barter with other Indians who in turn had secured them from the Chesepians.

If black pearls, and rumors of white ones, stirred the hearts and minds of the settlers, imagine their reaction to the stories of gold in the mountainous lands to the west, beyond the far reaches of Albemarle Sound. This Lane had to see for himself. The resultant expedition, in a fleet consisting of the pinnace, the two double wherries, and assorted smaller craft, had all the trappings of a ceremonial procession, with stopovers at each village along the way. They came first to the territory already visited by Amadas, north of Albemarle Sound. This was Weapemeoc, the land of King Okisko, later to become the North Carolina counties of Camden, Pasquotank, Perquimans, and Chowan.

For the most part the villages were located on or near the rivers that flowed into Albemarle Sound. From the written descriptions and the various contemporary maps it is possible to make only an educated guess as to their locations, but the villages he visited were probably in the following areas: Pasquenoke, "The Woman's Town" (Pasquotank River); Chepanoc or Chypanum (Little River); Weapemeoc (near Hertford, on the Perquimans River); Muscamunge (Yeopim River); and, finally, Mattaquen or Metackwem (Edenton Bay, near the site of one of North Carolina's colonial capitals).

The little flotilla turned north then, entering the wide, slow-moving Chawanoac (Chowan) River, which formed a natural dividing line between Okisko's territory of Weapemeoc and the next adjoining kingdom, Chawanoac, which Lane described as "the greatest Province and Seigniorie lying upon that river." They passed by a village Lane called "the blinde Towne, but the savages called it Ooanoke," and then, on the west bank of the Chowan in the general vicinity of today's Winton, they came to the Indian town of Choanoke. This town was city-sized when compared with Secotan and Pomeiooc and other towns they had visited, for it was "able to put 700 fighting men into the fielde" in addition to warriors from outlying sections of the province.

Impressed as he was with this largest of the Indian provinces and greatest of its towns, Lane reserved his choicest superlatives for the individual who held the territory together, Menatonon, king of Chawanoac. Menatonon was crippled—"A man impotent in his lims" was the way Lane described him—"but otherwise for a Savage, a very grave

and wise man." Lane was so impressed with King Menatonon's knowledge, "not onely of his owne Countrey, and
the disposition of his owne men, but also of his neigh-
bours round about him as wel farre as neere, and of the
commodities that eche Countrey yeeldeth," that he felt it
imperative to get from him as much information as possible before the expedition moved on. He accomplished
this by the simple expedient of taking the crippled king
prisoner.

In just two days, "when I had him prisoner with me,"
Lane was to report later, "he gave mee more understanding and light of the Countrey then I had received by all the
searches and salvages that before I or any of my companie
had had conference with." Menatonon showed him some
pearls that he had acquired earlier from the king of a powerful nation occupying a vast territory to the northeast,
headquartered on an island in a large deep-water bay apparently connected with the open sea. Lane learned that
there was an established trade route between Menatonon's town of Choanoke and the bay kingdom—three
days of canoe travel up the Chowan River, then four days
overland to the bay itself. A plan began to take form in
his mind, a plan that would give him an opportunity to
search for a site for permanent settlement with a deep-
water harbor and possibly produce a source of valuable
pearls as well.

It was early spring, March, when Lane reached Choanoke and took Menatonon as his prisoner. Easter, the
target date for the return of Grenville with reinforcements, was less than a month away. Assuming that he
would then have several hundred additional men and a
variety of ships under his command, Lane decided to wait
until after Grenville's arrival before putting his plan into
effect. First, he said later, "I woulde have sent a small
Barke with two Pinnesses about by Sea to the Northwarde
to have found out the Bay he spake of, and to have
sounded the barre if there were any." At the same time he

would personally lead a force of some 200 men back to Choanoke and induce Menatonon to provide support for the boat trip up the Chowan and the overland trek to the bay. This size force would be needed since Lane planned to establish way stations along the route. The first of these intermediate bases would be an enclosed fortification to be erected on the banks of the Chowan at the point where the expedition moved inland. Leaving 25 or 30 men there to guard the boats, he would lead the expedition overland for two days, where he expected to find the site of an Indian village with fields of ripening corn at hand for his next small fort. Again leaving a guard detachment, he would then proceed on to the deep-water bay, where he planned to throw up a major installation, employing in this more formidable project not only the approximately 150 settlers remaining under his charge but a large number of Menatonon's best men as well.

The success of this plan was dependent on Menatonon's providing him with experienced guides, a large work crew, and adequate food for the expedition. As a means of ensuring the cooperation of the Chawanoac leader, Lane took a second prisoner, Skiko, the "best beloved sonne" of Menatonon. He then sent the pinnace back to Roanoke Island, with his new prisoner under guard.

Before releasing Menatonon "upon a ransome agreed for," Lane pressed the crippled weroance for additional information about the territory to the west of Albemarle Sound, and what he learned was enough to set him off immediately in the direction of a fabled land of mountains and gold called Chaunis Temoatan, far up the river Morotico (Roanoke River). But first, Menatonon told him, he would have to pass through the territory of the Moratucks, a powerful nation occupying the land south of the river. Beyond the Moratucks, still farther to the west, were the Mangoaks, in whose domain Chaunis Temoatan was located.

With some thirty men in two boats, his own double

wherry and another he referred to as the "light horseman," Lane sailed back down the calm Chowan to the head of Albemarle Sound and began the slow ascent of the Roanoke. It was no easy task.

"Whereas the River of Choanoke, and all the other sounds, and Bayes, salt and fresh, shewe no currant in the world in calme weather, but are mooved altogether with the winde," Lane wrote, "this River of Morotico hath so violent a currant from the West and Southwest, that it made me almost of opinion that with oares it would scarse be navigable." But he pressed on, fighting the current of the spring thaw mile after laborious mile. As if the passage up that serpentine river against the torrents of onrushing water were not enough to try the mettle of the most hardy of his men, Lane made an almost fatal miscalculation. He had left Choanoke with food for only a few days, assuming that he could secure additional supplies from the Moratucks and the Mangoaks. But somehow the Moratucks had been forewarned that these strangely attired white-skinned beings were conquerors and not friendly travelers, and day after day, as Lane's expedition pressed onward and westward, no Indians were seen. Occasionally, fires were spotted along the shore, but on landing they invariably found that the natives had fled, leaving no food behind. Indian villages, likewise abandoned, were stripped clean of anything that might satisfy the gnawing in the bellies of the colonists.

Finally, with "but two dayes victuall left," and having neither met any Indians nor found so much as a single "graine of corne in any of their Townes," and according to his calculations being some "160 miles from home," Lane called a halt. He then proceeded to inform "the whole companie of the case wee stoode in for victuall, and of mine opinion that we were betrayed by our owne Savages." He thereupon advised his men that he "thought it good for us to make our returne homeward." But the adventurers accompanying Lane had heard wondrous stories of Chaunis Temoatan, and to a man they seemed affected with a common disease—gold fever.

"I willed them to deliberate all night upon the matter," Lane later reported, and the following morning he put it to a vote. "Their resolution fully and wholly was (and not three found to be of the contrary opinion) that whiles there was left one halfe pinte of corne for a man, that we should not leave the search of that River." A key point in their reasoning was the fact that they had with them two large dogs, bull mastiffs, used primarily for fighting and as watch dogs. If the corn ran out, they agreed, they could kill the dogs and prepare a "pottage" of sassafras leaves and fresh dog meat. Thus fortified, they could "live two dayes, which time would bring them downe the currant to the mouth of the River, and to the entrie of the sound," where they hoped to be able to take fish from the weirs of the Indians of Weapemeoc.

So the indomitable explorers pressed on against the current of the flooded Roanoke River. When they had eaten their final meager reserve of corn and become weakened and emaciated in both body and resolve, they heard at last the voices of Indians, calling to each other in the distance. Immediately, the forward motion was stopped, as the exhausted men listened intently for the welcome sounds. Manteo, riding in the lead boat with Lane, was instructed to answer the calls. "They presently began a song, as we thought in token of our welcome to them," Lane said, but then, suddenly, Manteo "betooke him to his peece, and tolde mee that they ment to fight with us." The words were hardly spoken when the attack came, a volley of arrows, striking the boats, but inflicting "no hurt, God be thanked, to any man." Lane's men responded with gunfire, and the awesome sound, if not the shot, dispersed the attackers. That was enough for Lane. His men landed, briefly searched the surrounding woods, and then, with night falling, prepared a sheltered camp ashore, "making a strong corps of garde, and putting out good centinels," including in all probability the two mastiffs.

The dogs, companions and guardians, were called on for double duty there on the riverbank far up the Roanoke in the land of the Moratucks—guard duty that night and breakfast the following morning. Their hacked up remains provided flavor for the bland pottage of sassafras leaves and sustenance for the men. Early the next day the two small craft began the descent of the Roanoke. They laid over that night on an island in the middle of the river and reached the broad sound the following evening. During the trip the entire force subsisted on the remnants of a "pottage of sassafras leaves, the like whereof for a meate was never used before as I thinke."

Even the elements seemed to have turned against them, for when they finally reached the sound, "the winde blewe so strongly, and the billow so great, that there was no possibilitie of passage without sinking of our boates." They were forced to ride at anchor for a full day, and by that time even their supply of sassafras and dogmeat stew was exhausted. It was "Easter eve," and good Christians that they were, the men "fasted very trulie."

Their luck turned then, and the next morning, "the wind coming very calme," they entered the sound. That afternoon they reached the Indian village of Chepanoc, where, as they had hoped, they were able to catch some fish and stave off starvation. The men feasted on fresh fish that evening, then resumed their voyage. The following morning they reached Roanoke Island and "home," still hungry but thankful to be alive.

It was Monday, the day after Easter, when they returned at last from their exploration of the Chowan and the Roanoke. The target date for the arrival of Grenville with his relief vessels had come and gone. They were still alone in this wilderness—alone, hungry, and no doubt despondent, for no English ships had appeared.

MAP 4. *Raleigh's Virginia. Engraving by Theodor de Bry from a drawing by John White.*

CHAWA
NGOI
OK
A

Ramushonuk
Ohanooock
Catokinge
Waratan
Mascoming
Chepanu
WEAPE
MEOC
Skicoak
Chesepiooc
Chesepiooc sinus
Apasus
Comokee
Pasquenoke
Trinety harbor

OCCIDENS
MERIDIES — SEPTENTRIO
ORIENS

Americæ
pars, Nunc Virginia
dicta primum ab Anglis
inuenta, sumtibus Dn Walteri
Raleigh, Equestris ordinis viri
Anno Dñi M D LXXXV regni vero
Sereniss. nostræ Reginæ Elisabethæ
XXVII
Huius vero Historia peculiari
Libro descripta est, additis
etiam Indigenarum
Iconibus

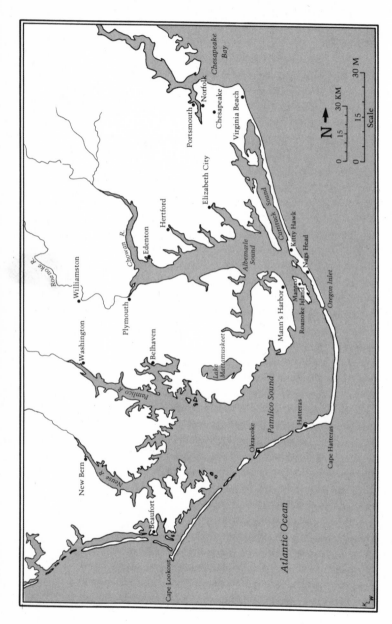

MAP 5. *Modern map of Raleigh's Virginia.*

CHAPTER 10

The Saga of Wingina

Even today, four centuries later, it is possible to have some sort of feeling for what must have gone through Ralph Lane's mind when he returned from his harrowing experience in the land of the Moratucks and Mangoaks the day after Easter only to learn that Grenville's relief vessels had failed to arrive at the expected time. But what of Wingina? What were the thoughts of this royal leader of the Roanoacs, this chief weroance of coastal Carolina in Elizabethan Virginia, when these alien beings came to claim his native land?

We have only contradictory accounts of this Indian king, and especially of his attitude toward the English visitors and his response to their sometimes autocratic and erratic behavior. Arthur Barlowe reported that Wingina was gravely ill when he and Amadas first reached the Carolina coast in the summer of 1584—"sore wounded in a fight which he had with the King of the next Countrey," was the way Barlowe phrased it. He had been "shotte in two places through the bodye, and once cleane thorough the thigh," and was recuperating at the "chiefe Towne of the Countrey," located six days' journey from Roanoke Island. For that reason Barlowe's contact was with Wingina's brother, Granganimeo, and he never saw the Indian king.

By the time Lane arrived a year later, Wingina had recovered from his wounds and returned to his Roanoke Island village. Lane pictured him as devious and hostile, and devoted a considerable part of his report to what he described as a conspiracy among the Indians, instigated by Wingina. On the other hand, Thomas Hariot saw the Roanoac weroance in a considerably different light, as a wise and deeply religious man, friendly and cooperative in his initial dealings with the colonists. The truth, no doubt, lies somewhere in between these extreme characterizations, and probably closer to Hariot's description than to Lane's, for the governor of Virginia had to find a way to justify his failure to carry out the specific mission assigned to him, and Wingina could have seemed a convenient scapegoat. From these widely divergent depictions, however, it is still possible to gain some understanding of and feeling for this Indian ruler of the land Raleigh's colonists claimed as theirs in the name of Queen Elizabeth and God.

Four men in the Indian hierarchy in the coastal Carolina area had special influence with Wingina and the course of action he eventually followed. One was his father, Ensenore, aged and probably infirm, from whom Wingina had inherited his mantle of authority. The second was his brother, Granganimeo, appropriately wise and regal, who ruled the little kingdom well when Wingina was incapacitated. The other two, though of lesser rank, were Manteo and Wanchese.

We might have a clearer picture if only we could learn more about the experiences of Manteo and Wanchese during their long stay in England. We have, however, only shady hints that the two reacted quite differently to what they saw and learned in England. On returning to Roanoke Island, Wanchese, it seems, took up residence again in the Indian town, close to his monarch, and we have only peripheral references to him thereafter. Manteo, on the other hand, seems to have been more taken with the ways of the whites; he became a sort of confidant, a combination guide, translator, and adviser. It is logical to assume that Wanchese was closely bound to Wingina, possibly even by kinship, while Manteo, born and raised on Croatoan, farther down Pamlico Sound (the supposed Sea of Verrazano), was probably from another tribe and family, aligned with the king of the Roanoacs only in a loose confederation.

Certainly, by the time Grenville reached the Outer Banks, Manteo occupied a position of trust, for it was Manteo, and not Wanchese, who was mentioned as having accompanied the general on his expedition to Secotan, Aquascogoc, and Pomeiooc; and it was Manteo, and not Wanchese, who was dispatched to Roanoke Island to inform Wingina that the white men had returned from across the sea.

Grenville and his lieutenants were well aware of the initial reaction of these native Americans when Amadas and Barlowe first appeared on the scene a year earlier. Admiral Amadas, at least, remembered full well how Granganimeo, as the direct representative of his brother the king, had greeted him and his fellow explorers in all friendliness. He had obviously been awed by the mighty European ships and guns and other marvelous inventions but had been ever trusting and eager to provide assistance. Granganimeo's wife had further demonstrated this friendly attitude when Barlowe visited the Indian village on Roanoke Island. Certainly, both must have been carrying out the general policies, if not the specific instructions, of the immobilized Wingina.

Even so, there must have been some concern on the part of Grenville and Lane as to how Wingina would receive them. He no doubt had first-hand reports from Manteo and Wanchese and had learned of Grenville's action in burning the town of Aquascogoc over the alleged theft of a silver cup. But if Wingina's attitude had changed, there was no outward indication of it, for his people continued to provide the colonists with food and assistance and guidance. Yet it is difficult to imagine Wingina's not having some fresh reservations as to what kind of beings these were, and what they really wanted.

Hariot, the missionary, worked hard to convert the heathen chieftain. But Wingina's faith seemed forever wavering, strengthened one moment then weakened the next, as he encountered over and over successive evidences of immortality and then of human frailty in the Englishmen. On two occasions, Wingina was "so grievously sicke that he was like to die." Both times, according to Hariot, "as hee lay languishing, doubting of anie helpe by his owne priestes, and thinking he was in such daunger for offending us and thereby our god," the weroance "sent for some of us to praie and bee a meanes to our God." His reasoning, under such circumstances, was not only that the English God might allow him to live but that, if the time had come for him to die, then with God's permission he might "after death dwell with him in blisse."

Although Hariot claims he tried to discourage such thinking, some of the Indians had come to believe that the settlers were not mortal men but direct creations of their God. There were, after all, no women amongst them, so how else could they have come into being except by divine creation? And their instruments—their "sea compasses," their "perspective glasse," their "spring clocks that seeme to goe of themselves, and manie other things" —were so far beyond the comprehension of the untutored natives that "they thought they were rather the works of gods then of men."

At other times, Wingina's belief in the immortality of the colonists and their close connection with the maker was shaken. He probably learned from Manteo and Wanchese that there were women and children back in England. As the lean months of winter came and went, it was obvious also that these strangers needed regular sustenance in the form of food and drink, just as did the Indians. Moreover, they seemed almost totally incapable of providing such necessities for themselves, growing more and more dependent on Wingina and his people for fish, game, and dried corn. No such doubts appear to have bothered Wingina's aged father, Ensenore. From start to finish he seems to have been convinced that the colonists were the direct offspring of their gods, and in all probability were themselves lesser gods, possessing powers beyond those of mere human beings. Whenever Wingina appeared to question the immortality of the white men, Ensenore was there to lead him back into the fold.

Even the cynics among the natives must have had second thoughts when it became obvious what was happening each time the colonists left a village in which they had not been properly received. Hariot recounted it in these words: "There was no towne where wee had any subtile devise practised against us, we leaving it unpunished or not revenged . . . but that within a few dayes after our departure from everie such towne, the people began to die very fast." Modern observers attribute this to epidemics of diseases introduced into America by the Europeans. Smallpox was one possibility, or measles, or maybe even the common cold and attendant pneumonia, against which the natives had no resistance.

Relations between the natives and the colonists had deteriorated to a new low by the time Lane embarked on his expedition to Albemarle Sound and beyond in early spring. The Indians employed runners to maintain constant communication within and between the various tribes and kingdoms. These were sturdy young men, probably specially trained to carry messages. Four of Wingina's men, including Manteo and Eracano, husband of the weroance's sister, accompanied Lane on his westward trek, and it is quite possible that runners kept Wingina posted on Lane's activities, including the capture of Menatonon. Certainly, Wingina was aware of Lane's actions by the time the pinnace returned to Roanoke Island with the prisoner, Skiko. And Lane was to claim later that Wingina instigated the conspiracy by which he and his fellow explorers were denied food by the Moratucks and Mangoaks. The plan, he said, was to let the colonists die of starvation, thus proving that they were not immortal.

If, in truth, Wingina was the mastermind behind this plan, then it can be assumed that his father, Ensenore, did not approve of the course being taken. Ensenore maintained that starvation would make no difference at all, for the Englishmen were in fact dead men returned to life, and death yet again would only result in the colonists' being able to "doe them more hurt." This view was shared by only a few others of the Indians, for Ensenore's chief ally in advocating a policy of continued friendship and cooperation with the settlers, Granganimeo, had died.

Wingina must have been surprised and shocked when Lane returned safely to Roanoke Island the day after Easter. So also was Menatonon, who shortly thereafter sent a messenger bearing what Lane thought was a present of pearls. But when he realized that these were intended as ransom for the release of Skiko, he refused to accept them and kept the young Chawanoac prince in shackles. Menatonon then sent a sizable delegation to Roanoke Island, including representatives of Okisko, king of Weapemeoc, this time seeking Skiko's release in exchange for assurances that "from that time forwarde hee, and his successours were to acknowledge her Majestie their onely Soveraigne."

Any hopes Wingina may have had for broad-based, unified action against Lane were shattered by this offer to compromise on the part of his powerful neighbors, Menatonon and Okisko. Lane still refused to release Skiko, however, and when Wingina called his weroances together for a council, the views of Ensenore once more prevailed. The Roanoacs proceeded to set out special weirs for the settlers, and to plant an area large enough, in Lane's view, to feed his whole company for a year. Wingina went even further, providing an extra plot of ground in which the Englishmen could plant their own crops.

But it was still only early April, and the corn harvest could not be expected until July. "All our feare," Lane said, "was of the two moneths betwixt," for if the Indians did not provide them with food from their own diminished larder, "wee might very well starve, notwithstanding the growing corne." Lane likened the situation to "the starving horse in the stable" surrounded by fields and meadows of lush grass. So he put even greater pressure on Wingina to assure an adequate supply of food. Once more, Wingina seemed to waver; he had hardly enough reserve for his own people, let alone for more than one hundred nearly starving intruders. Then, on April 20, the one restraining voice was stilled—the aged Ensenore died, and Wanchese appeared to emerge as a new power behind Wingina. If Lane's account is to be believed, the governor still had access to the inner circle of the Roanoke council. According to Lane, the conduit was his prisoner Skiko, the favored son of Menatonon, who had remained friendly with his captors, and even appreciative of having the opportunity to share room and board, meager as they were, with the godlike white men.

From this unlikely source, Lane claimed, he had received detailed information on a new plot against him hatched by Wingina and Wanchese. Wingina, who had changed his name to Pemisapan "upon the death of his brother Granganimo," was said to be in the process of uniting all of the chief weroances of the surrounding tribes, not only the Weapemeocs and Chawanoacs but the Moratucks and Mangoaks as well, in a conspiracy to destroy the white men. They were to assemble a force of some seven or eight hundred "bowes" from the territory above Albemarle Sound and seven hundred additional warriors from more distant tribes, including even the Chesepians, to launch a massive attack on the English stronghold on Roanoke Island.

Lane even claimed to have secured from Skiko the details of the plan of battle. Lane himself was to be the first target. Two of Wingina's "principall men," Tarraquine and Andacon, "with twentie more appointed to them had the charge of my person," and "in the dead time of the night" were to "beset my house." Their first act would be to "put fire in the reedes, that the same was covered with," assuming that "my selfe woulde have come running out of a sudden amazed in my shirt without armes, upon the instant whereof they woulde have knocked out my braynes."

Similar attacks were to be launched almost simultaneously against Hariot and the "rest of our better sort, all our houses at one instant being set on fire as afore is sayde," and the buildings in the nearby fort as well. To ensure that the colonists were in a weakened condition at the time of the attack, Lane further claimed, the Indians planned to refuse, for several weeks prior to that time, to "sell us any victuals whatsoever" and each night to "have our weares robbed." This would make it necessary for Lane to disband his company "into sundry places to live upon shell fishe," as "the Savages themselves doe." Thus weakened and dispersed, the colonists would be easy prey.

Whether or not credence can be given to Lane's version, the fact is that he did find it necessary to disperse his small force. Twenty men, under Captain Stafford, were sent to Croatoan, Manteo's home near modern Cape Hatteras, not only to search for their own food and sustenance but "also to keepe watch, if any shipping came upon the coast to warne us of the same." Ten more men, under Master Pridiox, were sent in the pinnace to Hatarask (now Pea Island), on the Outer Banks just below the lower end of Roanoke Island, also to watch for shipping. And every week he sent yet another detachment of between sixteen and twenty men "to the mayne over against us" to live off roots and oysters and whatever food they could scrounge.

According to Lane, this whole business was carried on by both sides in a manner of which modern politicians and diplomats would be proud. On the surface relations were made to appear friendly, with lines of communication kept open in much the same way that the president of the United States and the head of the government in the Soviet Union keep their diplomats going back and forth, with their telephone hot lines always at the ready.

This was demonstrated when Lane had word, through Skiko, that the warriors from the outlying tribes were planning to assemble at Roanoke Island. So he devised a plot of his own. "I sent to Pemisapan to put suspition out of his heade," Lane wrote, "that I ment presently to goe to Croatoan, for that I had heard of the arival of our fleet, (though I in trueth had neither heard nor hoped for so good adventure) and that I meant to come by him, to borrow of his men to fish for my company, and to hunt for me at Croatoan, as also to buy some foure dayes provision to serve for my voyage."

The reply from Wingina, according to Lane, was that he himself would come to Roanoke Island from his new headquarters at Dasamonquepeuc (near our Manns Harbor, on the mainland). "But from day to day hee deferred," so Lane decided to move forward with the culmination of his own plan. He ordered his men to gather up all of the Indian canoes they could find on the island, in which process the English soldiers "met with a Canoa, going from the shoare, and overthrew the Canoa, and cut off 2. savages heads." Indian observers on shore witnessed this action, "whereupon the cry arose" and a pitched battle ensued. "Some three or foure of them at first were slayne with our shot, the rest fled into ye woods." It was late evening then, and under cover of darkness that night Lane crossed the sound to Dasamonquepeuc with a force of some twenty-five men.

Wingina's emissaries met Lane at the landing below Dasamonquepeuc, and he sent word to the Indian king that he was going to Croatoan, but he wanted first to complain that one of Wingina's weroances, Osocon, had the night before released his prisoner Skiko, "whom I had there present tied in an handlocke." The ruse seemed to work, and Wingina agreed to let Lane and his men enter the village. The question, of course, is this: If Wingina even then was bringing to fruition his master conspiracy in which more than a thousand warriors were assembling for a final attack on the English colonists, then why would he have allowed an armed force of the enemy to enter his village without taking the necessary precautions against a surprise attack? This adds weight to the later contention by Hariot that Lane's tale of a conspiracy was largely a fabrication.

Seven or eight of Wingina's weroances, "not regarding any of the common sort," were assembled in the village when Lane's force entered Dasamonquepeuc. No doubt Wingina and his lieutenants were seated on mats, as was the Indian custom when receiving visitors, and, Lane, never one to ignore an opportunity at hand, sounded the prearranged signal for the attack, shouting the words "Christ our victory." His soldiers opened fire, with devastating effect. Wingina, one of the first struck by the gunfire, fell to the ground as if dead. Lane then turned his attention to "the saving of Manteos friends," who had accompanied his invading force, and was not immediately aware that Wingina had jumped to his feet and run away as though he had not been wounded. The soldiers took to the woods in hot pursuit, but it was Lane's personal servant, the Irishman Nugent, who became the hero of the day— for it was he who overtook the fleeing Wingina and returned presently carrying the king's head.

Wingina, king of the Roanoacs, was dead. Ensenore, his father, "the only frend to our nation that we had amongst them," was dead. Granganimeo, he of the stately demeanor, described by Barlowe as "mannerly, and civill, as any of Europe," was dead.

Lane had won the battle. But in the process had he lost the war?

CHAPTER 11

Sir Francis Drake to the Rescue

Ralph Lane had no way of knowing it, of course, but at the very moment that his personal servant, Edward Nugent, was emerging from the woods at Dasamonquepeuc carrying the head of King Wingina in his hand, more than thirty English vessels were en route to Roanoke Island with supplies and reinforcements.

Raleigh and Grenville had encountered difficulty in putting together the relief effort, partly because the queen's enthusiasm for the venture had seemed to cool. It was therefore necessary for them to raise more funds from private sources. By Easter—the time Lane understood they were to have reached Roanoke Island—no vessels had left England, and it was obvious that Grenville would not be ready to depart for at least several more weeks. Accordingly, Raleigh hurriedly arranged to send a single ship with adequate supplies to tide Lane's colonists over until the main relief force could reach the Outer Banks.

Much closer at hand, however, was a truly massive English fleet. Having completed a series of successful raids against Spanish bases in the West Indies and Florida, Sir Francis Drake was about ready to head back to England, and he had planned a stopover at Roanoke Island to find out how Raleigh's colonists were faring. In January, Drake had sacked the Spanish stronghold of Santo Domingo in the first of his series of bold attacks on Spain's New World outposts. On June 1, the date of Lane's Dasamonquepeuc massacre, he was conducting mopping-up operations at Saint Augustine after capturing both the fort and the town and routing the inhabitants.

Just one week later, Captain Stafford, foraging for survival at Cape Hatteras, where he had been sent by Lane to be on the lookout for relief vessels, sighted a number of ships offshore. He must have had some serious doubts as to whether this was in fact an English fleet, for he counted no less than twenty-seven craft, and it was unlikely that Raleigh could have put together such a flotilla. But Stafford and his men were hungry—nearly starved in fact—and prospects for survival in Virginia, especially after the affair at Dasamonquepeuc, must have seemed bleak indeed. Capture by Spaniards, if this proved to be a Spanish fleet, could be no worse a fate than being abandoned in this alien land. So Stafford sent his men down toward the beach to light signal fires.

Hallelujah! As small boats pulled away from the ships and approached the shore, it was obvious to the lookouts that the occupants were Englishmen, not Spaniards. They held a brief conference there on the beach at Hatteras, and it was decided that the fleet would move up the coast, cautiously, and anchor offshore opposite Port Ferdinando. Stafford would hurry back to Roanoke Island with the glorious news that help had arrived at last.

Stafford reported to the governor the following day, June 9. On June 10 the lookouts on the banks opposite Roanoke Island sent word that the fleet had arrived and anchored offshore. On the next day, Lane visited Drake on board his flagship and recounted his version of the events of the winter and spring.

Drake was a man of action, and not one to dawdle long when decisions were to be made. According to the journal of his voyage he offered Lane a clear-cut choice. He would leave him a ship and one or more small boats manned by experienced masters and mariners, plus enough additional supplies for another month of exploration in the area before having to make a final decision on whether to abandon the Roanoke Island base. Or, if Lane and his fellow settlers "thought they had made sufficient discoverie alreadie, and did desire to return into England, he would give them passage."

Lane called together his principal officers and gentlemen, and the answer was soon forthcoming. They would accept the first offer and remain at Roanoke Island, at least long enough to see if Grenville showed up with the promised reinforcements.

Specific details were soon worked out. A number of Lane's men, those he described as "weake, and unfit men for my good action," were to be transferred to one of Drake's ships and taken back to England. Able-bodied replacements from among the various vessels were to be left with Lane in exchange. In addition to the promised food, Drake would provide Lane with small guns, as well as "handweapons, match and lead, tooles, apparell, and such like." As for vessels, Lane reported later that he was offered a 70-ton bark, *Francis*, plus "two fine pinnaces, and 4. small boats." Any question as to how Lane's "Admirall," Philip Amadas, could handle this windfall of shipping was resolved when two of Drake's most experienced captains, Abraham Kendall and Griffith Herne, agreed to remain behind and serve as masters of the vessels assigned to Lane.

For the next few days there was frenzied activity aboard the twenty-seven vessels of Drake's fleet riding at anchor off Port Ferdinando. Supplies and equipment had to be assembled and loaded on *Francis* and the two pinnaces. Men had to be selected as replacements for those among Lane's colonists who were too weak or otherwise unfit for "good action." After a year of separation from other Europeans there were stories to tell and adventures to recount, as Lane's officers and gentlemen, and the soldier-colonists as well, rested aboard the ships, nourishing their shrunken bellies and bodies back to normal.

How quickly the forces of nature can alter the best-

FIGURE 13. *Sir Francis Drake (courtesy of the North Carolina Division of Archives and History).*

made plans of mere human beings. Four centuries ago, as today, the waters off the Outer Banks of North Carolina were a frequent target of those awesome cyclonic storms that make up slowly in the South Atlantic, churn through the Caribbean, then curve gradually northward past Cape Hatteras into the North Atlantic. It was mid-June, 1586, and the hurricane season was at hand.

On June 13 "there arose a great storme," the Drake journal recorded, "that lasted three dayes together, and put all our Fleete in great daunger, to be driven from their ankoring upon the coast." Under such stress the man-made cables could not hold, and the larger vessels "were driven to put to sea in great daunger, in avoiding the coast, and could never see us againe untill we met in England." An observer on one of Drake's vessels, *Primrose*, said that the storm brought "thunder . . . and raigne with hailstones as Bigge as hennes egges" and "greate Spowtes at the seas as thoughe heaven & [earth] woulde have mett."

By June 16 the hurricane had passed, and Drake and Lane took stock. *Francis*, the ship assigned to Lane, had disappeared, her fate unknown, apparently with several of Lane's key lieutenants aboard. Most of the smaller vessels that were to have been left with the colonists had been wrecked. Supplies on the remaining ships were now drastically limited. And Drake's captains and seamen seemed to have second thoughts about remaining behind on this exposed coast, thus risking the possibility of losing their shares of the loot from the highly successful Spanish raids.

But Drake had a stake in the Roanoke Island venture, not necessarily as an investor, but certainly as one whose grand plan for challenging Spanish power in America hinged to a certain degree on the establishment of fortified English bases along the coast above Florida. Once again he gave Lane a choice. He would leave him a single vessel, with a limited though just share of his drastically depleted reserves of food and supplies, or he would transport the colonists back to England. *Francis*, the 70-ton bark, was no longer available, having disappeared in the storm; nor could Drake provide Lane with even a single pinnace or small boat. In fact, the only vessel he could spare was the 170-ton bark *Bonner*. This craft was so large that there was no possibility of its being able to enter the inlet, and it would have to remain at anchor well offshore.

Drake, said by one biographer to have been "as politically discerning as he was navigationally brilliant," was well aware of the importance of the decision facing Lane, and of possible reactions back in England if it was decided to abandon the base on Roanoke Island. He therefore insisted that Lane's answer be put in writing and signed not only by the governor but by all of his chief advisers as well. There was urgency, too, for Drake was anxious to be quit of this dangerous coast. In all of his years of brilliant accomplishment at sea this must have been a new experience for him. He was, after all, England's greatest living naval hero, already the first English captain to have reached the Pacific Ocean, the first European of any nationality to explore the Pacific coast of Canada, and the first Englishman successfully to circumnavigate the globe. In the preceding few days off the Outer Banks he had, as Lane pointed out, "in that storme sustained more perill of wracke then in all his former most honourable actions against the Spaniards."

He need not have worried, for Lane's answer was not long in coming. Word of the offer had spread quickly throughout the fleet, and by the time the governor was able to assemble "such Captaines and Gentlemen of my companie as then were at hand" all of them were, in his words, "as privie as my selfe to the Generals offer." The evidence was weighed, and all indicators pointed in a single direction. Lane listed the points in concise language: "The weaknesse of our companie, the small number of the same, the carying away of our first appointed barke, with those two especiall masters" and "our principall provisions in the same"; and, finally, "our hope for supplie with Sir Richard Grenvill, so undoubtedly promised us before Easter, not yet come, neither then likely to come this yeere." He made no mention of trouble with the Indians; nor did he need to, for every man under his command was well aware of the possible results of his high-handed actions were they to remain.

In any event, he implied, the final decision was not theirs to make, for the Almighty had already done that for them. "The very hand of God," it seemed, was "stretched out to take us from thence."

The document was quickly drawn, signed, and delivered to Drake, but other problems still remained. Small boats had to be sent back to Roanoke Island "for the fetching away of fewe that there were left with our baggage." But even this proved difficult, for the weather was still "boysterous" in the wake of the hurricane, and the pinnace dispatched to Roanoke Island was steered by men who had never before sailed those shallow sounds or navigated the treacherous Outer Banks inlets, and the little vessel ran aground again and again. Returning through the inlet, the heavily overloaded pinnace struck a submerged shoal and was almost capsized. Obviously, the seamen, already described by Lane as being "much agrieved with their long and daungerous abode in that miserable road," were more interested in saving their boat and their lives and making it safely back to the vessels riding at anchor offshore than in worrying about the personal possessions of the colonists. Accordingly, to lighten the grounded pinnace, all excess baggage including "all our Cardes, Bookes and writings, were by the Saylers cast over board." Presumably, the items jettisoned included Hariot's chronology and many of White's drawings.

Such was the haste of the departure that three of Lane's men, off somewhere fending for themselves when Drake's fleet arrived, could not be located. There was no time to search for them, so the three were left behind—the first "lost colonists" of Roanoke Island.

The vessels of Drake's patched-up fleet, with Lane's remaining colonists on board, weighed anchor and departed the coast on June 18. Even as they headed northward to take advantage of the prevailing winds and currents, Raleigh's single relief vessel was approaching the Outer Banks from the south. Information on the voyage of this 100-ton craft is sketchy, though there is evidence that it left English waters in early April, shortly after Easter. If so, its passage was uncommonly slow, for Lane did not leave with Drake until the third week in June, some two and a half months later. Had the vessel reached its destination more expeditiously with relief for Lane, the continuity of settlement on Roanoke Island would, in all probability, have been maintained.

Of all the accounts of the Raleigh expeditions published by Hakluyt, the only ones that are not personal narratives are the brief report on the voyage of this single vessel, and of Grenville's small fleet, in the spring and summer of 1586. The author is unknown, but he must have gotten his information from someone other than Lane, for that part of the report dealing with the abandonment of Roanoke Island is highly critical of the governor. The colonists, the account states, "left all thinges so confusedly, as if they had bene chased from thence by a mightie armie, and no doubt so they were, for the hande of God came upon them for the crueltie, and outrages committed by some of them against the native inhabitantes of that Countrie."

The exact date of the arrival of this vessel on the Outer Banks is not recorded; the Hakluyt account states only that "immediatly after the departing of our English Colonie out of this paradise of the worlde, the shippe above mentioned sent and set forth at the charges of Sir Walter Ralegh, and his direction, arrived at Hatorask." Neither are we provided with any information at all concerning how long the vessel remained off the Outer Banks or exactly what was done while the ship was there. The whole period is covered in a single phrase: "after some time spent in seeking our Colony up in the Countrie, and not finding them," the expedition "returned with all the aforesayd provision into England."

Time and again, in reviewing the story of the first colony, questions arise for which there are no clear answers. The obvious question in this instance is why the captain of the relief vessel, who was aware that Grenville was following him in a more fully equipped fleet, did not wait longer for the general to arrive. The idea of spending two and a half months on such a journey in a vessel loaded with supplies and then, after what seems only a cursory search, sailing back again to England with the vessel still fully loaded, seems inexplicable.

Grenville was, in fact, close behind. "Fourteene or fifteene daies after the departure of the aforesayd shippe," the account states, he reached the North Carolina coast with three "well appointed" vessels. Sir Richard had left England in late April with some four hundred men, but could not resist taking prizes even before he was clear of the home waters. He stopped an English ship, justifying his action by claiming that she had been engaged in illegal trade with Spain, and removed some wine and oil. He then encountered, and captured, two French vessels, which he sent back to England with prize crews, and took a Dutch flyboat reportedly bound for Spain.

Again, the printed account is sketchy, though historian Quinn has located a deposition by a Spanish pilot named Pedro Diaz, who had been captured by Grenville the preceding year and accompanied him on the 1586 expedition. The Diaz account sheds some additional light on the matter, but only enough to leave still more tantalizing and unanswered questions.

Grenville's fleet anchored off Port Ferdinando just above the northern end of Hatorask Island; then he headed for Roanoke Island in a small boat. He found the fort and settlement deserted, though Diaz claimed his men discovered the hanged bodies of an Englishman and an Indian.

The former was probably one of the three men left behind by Lane; the latter, one of the friendly Croatoans, if the Diaz account is to be believed. Grenville then traveled "up into divers places of the Countrey, as well to see if he could here any newes of the Colony left there by him the yere before, under the charge of Master Lane his deputie, as also to discover some places of the Countrie." In all of this exploration it appears that only three Indians were encountered, all of whom were captured, though two soon managed to escape. From the third Indian they "got an account of how Francisco Draque had brought away the people who had been on that island."

At last, then, Grenville was able to piece together a general outline of the events that had led to Lane's abandonment of the settlement. But he was now faced with a dilemma. Should he reestablish the settlement, leaving there as many as he could spare of the men remaining from the four hundred with whom he had left England, or should he forget the whole business and return to England with the supplies still stowed in the holds of his vessels? "After good deliberation," the account tells us, "unwilling to loose the possession of the Countrie, which Englishmen had so long helde," he decided to "leave some men behinde to retaine possession." But how many? A hundred or so, as with Lane? More? Less? In fact he proceeded to land only "15. men in the Ile of Roanoke furnished plentifully with all maner of provision for two yeeres, and so departed for England." How he arrived at that particular number must remain a mystery.

Who were these men? Pedro Diaz said that this group included "a Master Cofar, an Englishman, and another called Chapeman" in charge, and that Grenville left eighteen of them instead of fifteen. But beyond that we have no names or other information, and the only certainty is that as Drake's fleet, Raleigh's relief vessel, and Grenville's three ships headed back to England, somewhere between seventeen and twenty men, if the two survivors of the three left by Lane are included, remained behind in Virginia. In light of the "crueltie, and outrages" committed by Lane against the Indians, including the murder of Wingina, the prospects were not bright for the second attempt at English colonization in America.

CHAPTER 12

Men, Women, and Children

Sir Walter Raleigh must have had some second thoughts about his plan for American colonization when, one after another, Drake's fleet, the single relief vessel, and Grenville's three ships straggled back to England in the early fall of 1586. After three years of trying to put together expeditions to Wingandacon-Virginia, of raising money and fitting out ships, of trying to sign on sailors, soldiers, and would-be settlers, he seemed no closer to his goal than he was when Amadas and Barlowe had returned a full two years earlier with glowing reports of their discoveries. No gold or valuable commodities had been found. The Roanoke Island base was held by a pitifully small garrison. The once friendly relations with the native people had deteriorated to an alarming extent.

There was, however, some good news mixed in with the bad. After all, Ralph Lane's men had lived for nearly a year in this far distant heathen land, and Raleigh's claim had gone unchallenged by other princes of Christendom. Further, of Lane's 107 colonists, reportedly only 4 had died, and even those were individuals who were alleged to have been so feeble they should never have gone there in the first place. A large area from the Pamlico River on the south to Chesapeake Bay on the north, and as far west as the Piedmont, had been explored and mapped, and the written accounts of those discoveries by Grenville, Lane, and Hariot depicted a fertile and hospitable land, well suited for permanent settlement, with the added prospect of gold in the hills beyond. Finally, the tantalizing drawings of John White were enough to whet the appetite of anyone seeking adventure and a profitable new life beyond the seas.

Though many questions remained, one thing was certain: Roanoke Island was not a suitable location for a major and permanent English settlement in America, if for no other reason than its total lack of access to a protected deep-water harbor. Yet there were encouraging signs that such a harbor did exist a relatively short distance to the north, on the bay the Indians called Chesepiock. So far the venture had proceeded on a logical, though slow-paced, progression from the initial voyage of discovery to the establishment of a temporary military outpost, all the while bringing about increased familiarization with the native inhabitants, the land, and the resources. Had not the time come, finally, for the ultimate step, the establishment of a colony in fact as well as in name, a living, loving, breeding colony not just of explorers and soldiers but of men and women prepared to spend their lives and raise their families in far-off America? Raleigh obviously felt so.

Four centuries later, Sir Walter Raleigh is regarded as one of the most captivating figures in English-American history. Any man reputed to have spread his fancy cloak over a mud puddle so his queen would not soil her dainty feet is a man worth writing about. And historians and biographers have been writing about Raleigh for centuries, turning out hundreds upon hundreds of books and profiles in which each succeeding author tried to capture and convey a true feeling for this many-faceted Elizabethan. They have not had an easy time of it.

The problem has not been a lack of contemporary written material on Raleigh, however, for it abounds—in correspondence, legal documents, official government rec-

FIGURE 14. *Sir Walter Raleigh (courtesy of the North Carolina Division of Archives and History).*

ords, and the extensive writings of Raleigh himself. Rather, as biographer William Stebbing pointed out nearly ninety years ago, "the perplexities are numberless and distracting," for "never surely was there a career more beset with insoluble riddles and unmanageable dilemmas." After years of studying his subject, Stebbing complained that "at each step, in the relation of the most ordinary incidents, exactness of dates, or precision of events, appears unattainable. Fiction is ever elbowing fact, so that it might be supposed contemporaries had with one accord been conspiring to disguise the truth from posterity."

There is confusion from the very beginning, even over such basics as the date of his birth (either 1552 or 1554) and the spelling of his name (biographer Willard M. Wallace has found seventy-three different versions in use during his lifetime). Raleigh further confused the matter by spelling his own name several different ways. In time he grew more consistent, and from 1584 until his death in 1618, according to Wallace, "his signature on all correspondence was *Ralegh*, the name that also appears in his books." As for *Raleigh*, the spelling "which posterity has preferred," it is a usage the man himself is "not known to have ever employed."

The confusion and complexities go far beyond mere dates and names, however, for as Wallace points out, "few men in history have equalled him in the number and diversity of his interests. He was soldier, sailor, courtier, Captain of the Queen's Guard, businessman, explorer, colonizer, member of Parliament, devotee of science, ship designer, military engineer, musician, library patron, historian, and poet."

Physically, Raleigh was an imposing figure. Biographers J. H. Adamson and H. F. Folland describe him as "a tall man, a little over six feet in an age when the average height was nine inches less, and he was regally slim. He was handsome, too . . . with deep brown curly hair and a trim, pointed beard which lengthened his already elegantly narrow face. His features were sharp, his nose long, his lips firm but sensuous. And there was something strange about his eyes, 'pig-eyed' he had once been called," for his eyes were closely spaced and heavy lidded.

Raleigh dressed in "flamboyant elegance," with "bright jewels flashing from his fingers, his ears and his clothes." At ease in the presence of royalty, he "could be shifty, wheedling, whining," traits which did not necessarily endear him to those with whom he came in contact. "It is not surprising that such a man made few friends," Wallace states. "Indeed, in his drive toward wealth and fame, Raleigh became the most hated and feared Englishman of his time, . . . for women as well as men felt uncomfortable in the presence of this brilliant, ruthless, sardonic creature."

Born at Hayes Barton in Devon, he was the younger son of Sir Walter Raleigh of Budleigh and his third wife, Katherine Gilbert Raleigh. Young Walter was the half-brother of Sir Humphrey Gilbert, cousin of Sir Richard Grenville, and more distantly related to Sir Francis Drake. While still a teenager, he fought on the Protestant side in the French Wars of Religion. Later, he made some half-hearted attempts at acquiring a formal education before sailing as captain of *Falcon* in Gilbert's ill-fated first expedition in 1578.

After participating in action against Irish rebels in Munster, the tall, dashing, flamboyant Raleigh attracted the attention of his queen. By 1583 he had become a favorite at court, and Elizabeth provided him with "lucrative monopolies, properties, and influential positions," culminating in his receiving the Virginia grant and being knighted.

Raleigh's subsequent disfavor at the court of Queen Elizabeth can be traced to a secret marriage and the birth of a son in 1592. As a result both Raleigh and his wife, Elizabeth Throckmorton, were imprisoned in the Tower of London. By then the Virginia enterprise had run its course, but Raleigh still dreamed of leading the effort to colonize America with Englishmen. In 1595, after release from prison, he embarked on an expedition to the New World, but not to Virginia. His destination was South America, and on his return he wrote a book, *The Discoverie of Guiana*. He subsequently participated in an unsuccessful expedition against the Spanish city of Cadiz, and in 1600 he was appointed governor of Jersey, one of the Channel Islands.

The Elizabethan age ended in 1603 with the death of the Virgin Queen, and so did the rising fortunes of Sir Walter Raleigh. He and several others were soon charged with plotting against the new king, James I, and were tried, found guilty, and sentenced to death. Although he received a reprieve on that sentence, he was once again imprisoned in the Tower of London, where he was to spend much of the remainder of his life. Released again in 1616, and by then in his sixties, he made his final voyage to Guiana. Soon after he returned from that expedition, his suspended sentence was revoked, and on October 29, 1618, Raleigh was executed.

Only after his death did this "most hated and feared Englishman of his time" acquire the status he had sought in life. His writings, both prose and poetry, are now recognized as among the outstanding literary works of his time, and as biographer Wallace states, "generations who never knew the spell of his incisive, compelling personality or heard the sharp, arrogant voice speaking in a mouth-filling Devonshire accent have marveled that the greatness of Raleigh could have been so poorly appreciated by his contemporaries." The Virginia settlement, undertaken at the height of his power and influence with Queen Elizabeth, was probably his most important contribution to history. Its failure can be attributed at least in part to his concurrent involvement in so many other activities. Stebbing explains Raleigh's lack of recognition during his own lifetime: "Had he been less vivacious and many-sided," he wrote, "he might have succeeded better, suffered less, and accomplished more."

It is not known exactly when Raleigh's interest first began to be diverted from Virginia and the vast area covered by his North American patent to Guiana and South America. The time could well have been the winter of 1586–87, for by then some of those most closely involved with his colonization efforts seem to have had their fill of the venture. Philip Amadas, the original discoverer, and his partner Arthur Barlowe are heard from no more in the annals of the colonization effort. Ralph Lane, the first governor, and Sir Richard Grenville, the leader of the 1585 and 1586 expeditions, went on to other pursuits. Even Thomas Hariot, hard at work that winter on his book, which was to be the first written about America by an Englishman who had actually been there, had made his last voyage to Roanoke Island and Virginia. At least two others, however, were destined to play even more important roles in the drama still unfolding around Raleigh and his New World settlement: Simon Ferdinando, the pilot and master mariner, and John White, the artist.

White was the key, the individual on whose shoulders rested the responsibility for ultimate success or failure. He was, without question, a compassionate man, and, unlike Lane, an individual with a reverence for all of God's earthly creations, including even the natives of America, whom he had depicted in his drawings as people both gentle and proud. White was to be the governor of Raleigh's new and permanent colony in America.

The plan for this 1587 undertaking was quite different from those under which the Amadas-Barlowe, Lane, and Grenville expeditions had been launched. This attempt was to be much more closely attuned to Hakluyt's earlier concept of what was necessary for successful colonization in America. Women were to join their husbands this time, women and their children as well. And White set the proper example at the outset, as a leader should, for he took his pregnant daughter, Eleanor, with him to Virginia.

There were other easily discernible differences. These would-be colonists were to have an increased personal stake in the venture, investing their own savings where able or, at the very least, taking responsibility for outfitting themselves and their families. In exchange there were to be rewards and incentives—a grant of five hundred acres of land to the head of each household and a greater voice in government than that allowed in any of the prior English efforts, including Gilbert's—a first sweet taste of American democracy, if you will.

It is easy to speculate that the final arrangements for the expedition evolved gradually in discussions among a number of Raleigh's close associates, and that such discussions ranged from thoughtful and philosophical to animated. After all, these were men with divergent views who were improvising a strategy not only to extract wealth from America through colonization but to spread among the natives of those unsettled parts the true doctrine of Christianity, while at the same time dealing a potentially fatal blow to Spanish power in the New World.

When the time finally came to translate these ideas into formal written documents, it can be supposed that Hariot and Hakluyt both had a hand in the activity. The most meaningful contribution, however, probably came from White, whose enthusiasm for the venture could well have been the single most important factor in sustaining the necessary interest and momentum.

The basic document, signed January 7, 1587, created a "Bodye pollitique & Corporate" called "The Governour and Assistants of the Cittie of Ralegh in Virginea." Twelve assistants were named to serve with Governor White; of that number only one, Simon Ferdinando, appears to have visited Virginia previously. Little is known of the other assistants, though one of them was White's son-in-law, Ananias Dare, the husband of Eleanor White Dare. No copy of this basic agreement between Raleigh and the corporate directors of the Cittie of Ralegh has been located, but there are several references to it in subsidiary documents that have survived. One of these is "a patent of Arms" granted to the new governor and his assistants by the "chief officer of Armes of the moste noble order of the Garter."

The insignia for the newly created Cittie of Ralegh was to consist of a simple cross with a roebuck (a fully antlered buck deer) in the upper left corner. Equally undistinguished coats of arms were authorized, individually, for each of the twelve assistants. By Elizabethan standards at least, they were off to a good start.

In the basic agreement, White, it seems, was given primary responsibility for recruiting the colonists, probably with further inducements for those men whose wives were to accompany them and even more if they agreed to take their children as well. By mid-April three vessels were being readied for the passage to America: a 120-ton ship named *Lyon*, a flyboat, and a pinnace. When the little fleet finally set sail from Portsmouth on April 26, it was reported that 150 men had signed on as colonists, not counting wives and children and, apparently, some single women.

Two other passengers on White's vessels are mentioned only casually in the written accounts. These were Indians, natives of coastal Carolina who had been brought back to England by either Lane or Grenville the preceding fall. One was Towaye, who may have been the Indian captured by Grenville when he visited Roanoke Island and found the fort and settlement deserted. The other was Manteo, still friendly to the English despite Lane's brutal treatment of the Indians at Dasamonquepeuc. Having spent his second winter in England, again probably in Raleigh's household, Manteo seems to have so ingratiated himself with his host that Raleigh instructed White to install him as head of the deceased Wingina's domain when they returned to Roanoke Island.

By now the route and timetable for Raleigh's expeditions to the North Carolina coast had become established.

In 1584, in 1585, and again in 1586, his colonists had departed in late spring and followed a circuitous route south along the coast of Europe and northern Africa to the Canary Islands, then west to the Caribbean. Invariably they stopped over in the Spanish West Indies, to take on fresh water and food and often to search for Spanish prizes, before laying a course for the Florida coast, with a final leg northward to Cape Hatteras. They picked this particular time of year—and this specific route—to take advantage of the prevailing winds and the North Atlantic's clockwise currents, and because the route brought their vessels close to the Spanish shipping lanes. But it was still a long and drawn-out process, taking at least six weeks, and usually longer.

The departure of the three vessels from English waters, already later than had been customary for the prior crossings of the Atlantic, was delayed further when White made stops at the Isle of Wight and Plymouth after sailing from Portsmouth. It was thus May 8 when they finally cleared for the long crossing to the West Indies, a voyage that took forty-two days, some two weeks longer than had Grenville's in 1585. Apparently, they encountered bad weather off the coast of Portugal, for there is a single-sentence entry in White's report that reads, "The 16. Simon Ferdinando Master of our Admirall, lewdly foresooke our Flie boate, leaving her distressed in the Baye of Portingall."

This flyboat incident is the first mention of disagreement between Governor White and the most experienced of his assistants, the veteran mariner Ferdinando. How much credence can be given to continued criticism of the pilot in White's narrative is a matter for the individual reader to determine, though it must be kept in mind that Ferdinando left no papers in which his side of the disagreement was aired. The trouble between the two could have had its beginnings in Ferdinando's frustration over the delayed departure. Later on, White may have found in the pilot a convenient scapegoat for his own failures. In addition, historian Quinn points out, the two had an overriding difference in objectives. Both had a stake in the Cittie of Ralegh undertaking, but White's secondary interest was in observing and collecting natural history specimens for his drawings, while Ferdinando, the one-time pirate and privateer, undoubtedly was always hoping that he could return to England with rich prizes.

Three days after first sighting land in the Caribbean, *Lyon* and the pinnace came to anchor at St. Croix in the Virgin Islands, "where all the planters were set on land." Even experienced sailors need to stretch their legs on shore after six weeks of confinement in cramped quarters aboard a small vessel, and for the colonists, and especially the women and children, this must have been a joyous occasion. These were people unaccustomed to shipboard confinement and privation, and the lush and beautiful island of St. Croix must have seemed to them like heaven on earth.

Further, after six weeks at sea they undoubtedly hungered for fresh food, and there are indications that their water supply aboard ship had been so depleted that rationing had been necessary. Appropriately, therefore, one of their first actions upon reaching shore was to pick and eat the native fruit found growing wild and to drink fresh water wherever they could find it. The trouble was that the fruit they ate, similar in size and taste to small green apples, was poisonous, and all who sampled it were "fearefully troubled with a sudden burning in their mouthes, and swelling of their tongues so bigge, that some of them could not speake." So potent was the poison that one of the babies, "by sucking one of those womens breastes, had at that instant his mouth set on such a burning, that it was strange to see how the infant was tormented."

Fortunately, the effect from eating the applelike fruit was temporary, and in less than twenty-four hours had worn off. The water was another matter, however, for the only readily available supply was in a standing pond, and many of the colonists, so long limited to meager allotments of drinking water, sought relief in the pond from the burning sensation of the poisonous fruit. A number of them became ill from drinking from the pond, "the water whereof was so evill" that those who were more prudent and used it only to wash their faces awoke the next morning to find that "their faces did so burne, and swell, that their eies were shut up, and could not see in five or sixe daies or longer."

During the course of their three-day stay on St. Croix one of White's foraging parties discovered, "running out of a high rocke, a very faire spring of water," and for the time at least the water problem was taken care of. But they still needed fresh meat and salt, and while *Lyon* rode at anchor off St. Croix, the pinnace, with Edward Stafford serving as captain, was sent to the nearby island of Vieques "by Ferdinando, who assured him he should there finde great plentie of sheepe." Two days later *Lyon* caught up with the pinnace, whose crewmen had been unable to locate any sheep on Vieques, and together they sailed along the southern coast of Puerto Rico to the familiar haven at Muskito Bay. Three days were spent there in an effort fully to replenish the supply of fresh water, but again the colonists were dogged by bad luck (and possibly poor direction), for White claimed that so much beer was consumed at Muskito Bay that they ended up "spending in the meane time more beere, then the quantitie of the water came unto."

Two Irishmen, Darby Glande and Denice Carrell, were left behind at Muskito Bay; Glande contended later that he had escaped, having been forcibly impressed for service under White. Ferdinando headed for Rojo Bay in the hope of finding salt, as Lane had done under Grenville two years earlier. In preparation, the colonists had made a large number of special "sackes for that purpose." No doubt remembering the dissension between Lane and Grenville when the salt-taking activity at Rojo Bay had been threatened by armed Spaniards, Ferdinando apparently had a change of mind, possibly to avert another outbreak of hostility between himself and White. His most persuasive argument was that *Lyon* would be in danger of being wrecked if a storm arose on that exposed coast. White later contended that this was simply a ruse, stating that even as Ferdinando was trying to persuade him to leave Rojo Bay, "he caused the lead to be cast, and having craftily brought the shippe in three fathome, and a halfe water, he suddenly began to sweare, and teare God in peeces, dissembling great danger, crying to him at the helme, beare up hard, beare up hard: so we went off, and were disappointed of our salt, by his meanes."

Relations between White and Ferdinando were strained still further the following day when the governor wanted to go ashore on the west end of Puerto Rico to gather young fruit plants, including orange and pineapple, to be planted in Virginia, but was not allowed to do so. They then proceeded along the coast of Hispaniola toward the Caicos Islands, where, according to White, "Fernando saide were two salt pondes, assuring us if they were drie, wee might finde salt to shift with, until the next supplie." While some of White's men were searching for salt on one of the islands and others were hunting swan, Ferdinando, White said, "solaced himself a shoare, with one of the company," a statement that can be interpreted as implying that he engaged in sexual activity with one of the women. The others, meanwhile, were successful in their swan-hunting activity, but White wrote that Ferdinando's assurance that they would find salt on the island "prooved as true as the finding of sheepe" at Vieques.

In this state of open hostility between the two leaders of the expedition, they sailed from the Caicos Islands on July 7, headed at last for Virginia. The American mainland was sighted on July 16, when once again White accused the pilot of incompetence, deception, and dereliction of duty.

Specifically, he said that Ferdinando mistakenly thought he had reached the vicinity of Cape Hatteras, when in fact the land they sighted was much farther to the south. When he finally realized his error and put to sea, the two vessels "bare along the coast, where in the night, had not Captaine Stafforde bene more carefull in looking out, then our Simon Fernando, wee had beene all cast away upon the breache, called the Cape of Feare, for wee were come within two cables length upon it: such was the carelesnes, and ignorance of our Master."

At last, on July 22, *Lyon* and the pinnace arrived safely off the Outer Banks and anchored near the familiar Port Ferdinando opposite Roanoke Island. Raleigh's instructions were for them to make contact with the fifteen men left the previous summer by Grenville, and then proceed northward along the coast to their new home on Chesapeake Bay, where the "Cittie of Ralegh" was to be located. But subsequent events were to dictate a quite different course of action, resulting in yet another attempt to establish a settlement on Roanoke Island.

CHAPTER 13

The Cittie of Ralegh

The agreement between Sir Walter Raleigh and "the Governour and Assistants of the Cittie of Ralegh in Virginea" appears to have provided John White and his associates with unprecedented incentives for establishing new homes and new lives in America. In this it closely followed the earlier advice of Hakluyt, and it assumed that middle-class English families would be willing, even anxious, to sever all of their lifetime ties, disposing of their homesteads and accumulated assets in the process, in order to move some three thousand miles across the Atlantic to a new land of promise on the North American continent. To this day, their spiritual descendants in America have a tendency to take the same sort of chance in the search for a better life.

It should be understood that Raleigh did not cede to these colonists all his claims to America granted him under Queen Elizabeth's three-year-old patent. Rather, he was giving them the right to settle in one small portion only of what was then referred to as Virginia. He reserved the remainder for other ventures, including the maintenance of privateering bases, the extraction of gold from the interior, and even the establishment of other colonies. Thus the Cittie of Ralegh was intended to supplement, rather than replace, the other uses Raleigh had in mind for his vast domain.

The success or failure of the White colony was dependent on a variety of factors. At the very outset there was the question of whether enough families could be induced to join in the experiment. White may have hoped for even greater participation, but the fact that he signed up 150 men and a good representation of women and children attests to his ability as a recruiter. Supplies were another matter. Some have doubted whether the small fleet carried adequate provisions. In the designation of Simon Ferdinando as one of the assistants they at least had assurance—insofar as it was possible to have such assurance—that they would reach their destination safely, for the veteran navigator knew these waters as did no other man.

Unlike earlier voyages of exploration and efforts at exploitation under the Raleigh patent, the Cittie of Ralegh was to concentrate its energies on what might best be described as homesteading. In addition there was to be a determined effort to establish a friendly relationship with the native people—in short, a kind of permanent co-existence with the Indians. The deep-water port on Chesapeake Bay (today the site of Hampton Roads, the largest naval base in the world) would offer easy access for English vessels. The provision calling for a five-hundred-acre land grant to each family could serve as the foundation for an expanding agricultural economy. Also, continued maintenance of a privateering base at Roanoke Island, and the expected establishment of others along the coast, gave comfort to those concerned about the possibility of Spanish attacks.

The expanding role of England in challenging Spain's hold on the New World gave added promise that there would be frequent visits from British privateering squadrons, with the prospect of relief if emergencies arose, as had been provided Ralph Lane's colonists by Sir Francis Drake the year before. And always, of course, there was Sir Walter, back home in England, still concerned about the new colony in Virginia to which he had lent his name.

On paper, at least, even the corporate organization seemed well designed for the purpose, since, ideally, the twelve assistants would be individuals with diverse backgrounds, able to advise and consult with the governor before decisions were made. The one development no one seemed to anticipate was a clash of personalities among the leaders of the colony, as had occurred two years earlier between Grenville and Lane. Yet this is exactly what happened, and it changed the course of history.

The trouble between White and Ferdinando had been brewing almost from the time they set sail from England. Later, White was to charge that Ferdinando had deliberately abandoned the third vessel of the fleet, the flyboat, in the Bay of Portugal. He stole away in the darkness of night, White charged, hoping that the flyboat captain, Edward Spicer, who "never had beene in Virginia, would hardly finde the place," or better still would be captured by privateers or pirates before ever clearing European waters. White seemed convinced, even then, that Ferdinando was out to scuttle the project.

The final break came shortly after *Lyon* and the pinnace anchored off the Outer Banks on July 22, 1587. Governor White was understandably anxious to reach Roanoke Island as soon as possible, "hoping there to finde those fifteene Englishmen, which Sir Richard Greenvill had left there the yeere before." He was especially interested in learning how the fifteen had fared in dealings with the Roanoac Indians in light of Lane's Dasamonquepeuc attack. His plan was to confer with them and then "to returne againe to the fleete, and passe along the coast, to the Baye of Chesepiok, where we intended to make our seate and forte, according to the charge given us among other directions in writing, under the hande of Sir Walter Ralegh."

No sooner had White and "fortie of his best men" crowded aboard the pinnace, however, than instructions were shouted down from the ship to the sailors manning the little craft, "charging them not to bring any of the planters backe againe, but leave them in the Island, except the Governour, and two or three such as he approoved." The privateer's justification for this shocking and unexpected declaration, which amounted to open rebellion against White and direct violation of Raleigh's specific instructions, was that "the Summer was farre spent, wherefore hee would land all the planters in no other place."

If we are to believe White's journal—and in the absence of any other account of the incident there seems to be no alternative—Simon Ferdinando must have planned this move very carefully. Though White was the governor of the Cittie of Ralegh and Ferdinando only one of twelve assistants, in reality the mariner held the upper hand, for he was, after all, the admiral of the fleet, the master in name and in fact so long as the colonists were still aboard the vessels he commanded.

One can imagine White's feeling of helpless frustration and despair as he stood on the crowded deck of the little pinnace with the pick of his men surrounding him and heard these instructions shouted from the quarterdeck of *Lyon*. Did he yell back at Ferdinando above the sound of wind and wave? Did he argue with him, plead, try to change the pilot's mind, or at the very least seek some sort of reasonable compromise? Did he and his forty hand-picked colonists make any effort to convince the sailors manning the pinnace to ignore Ferdinando's instructions? We do not know, but it is of little consequence, for the matter was already decided. The sailors were Ferdinando's men, not White's. They had no direct interest in, no prospect of personal gain from, further dawdling with this colonization business when, under the experienced Ferdinando, there were bright prospects for successful privateering and prize taking in American waters—so long as the favorable weather of the summer months held out.

White was obviously a man able to face up to the

realities of the moment, and one capable also of adapting quickly to drastically changing circumstances. His journal covers the matter as succinctly as written words could, stating only that "it booted not the Governour to contend with them, but passed to Roanoake, and the same night, at Sunne set, went aland on the Island, in the place where our fifteene men were left."

The date was July 23, 1587, and it is an understatement of the first magnitude to say that it just was not John White's day. First, he was forced to accept a total change of plans for his colony, a change that meant he would have to settle again on Roanoke Island, at least temporarily, instead of seeking a new and better site for the Cittie of Ralegh on Chesapeake Bay. Then, as he and his fellow colonists searched for the members of Grenville's garrison in the failing light of dusk, he had another disappointment. Again, the journal entry is pithy and concise: "We found none of them nor any signe, that they had bene there, saving onely we found the bones of one of those fifteene, which the Savages had slaine long before."

Who among the colonists could have slept that first night in Virginia without being awakened repeatedly from frightful dreams of savagery and horror? White and forty of the most experienced men were ashore on Roanoke Island, or crowded together on the pinnace. The remaining men, and the women and children, were still cooped up on *Lyon*, little more than prisoners of the piratical Portuguese-Spanish pilot and his followers.

It behooved White to move rapidly, and he did. Early the next morning "the Governour, with divers of his companie, walked to the North ende of the Island, where Master Ralfe Lane had his forte, with sundry necessarie and decent dwelling houses, made by his men about it the yeere before, where wee hoped to finde some signes, or certaine knowledge of our fifteene men." But again they found only disappointment and failure. "When we came thither," the journal continues, "wee founde the forte rased downe, but all the houses standing unhurt." It was obvious that no one had inhabited these houses since winter, for the lower floors of the two-story structures "were overgrowen with Melons of divers sortes, and Deere within them, feeding on those Mellons: so we returned to our companie, without hope of ever seeing any of the fifteene men living."

It is easy, in retrospect, to give White low marks for competency as a governor and administrator, but once again he demonstrated an ability to respond to adversity with positive action. "The same day order was given," the entry in the journal reads, "that every man should be imploied for the repairing of those houses, which we found standing, and also to make other newe Cottages, for such as shoulde neede." The decision, therefore, was to take up residence again in the little community Lane had built on the north end of Roanoke Island, in proximity to his old fort, instead of spending the extra time and effort that would be involved in starting from the ground up at a new site. It is logical to assume that most of Lane's men, who lived there for nearly a year in 1585–86, had resided in communal dwellings, except for the governor, Hariot, and a few others of the gentlemen who had smaller houses of their own. The families, however, had quite different needs, necessitating the construction of a number of new houses. Just one day after first sighting the coast opposite Roanoke Island, construction had already been started on the buildings that would make up the temporary Cittie of Ralegh.

Two days later there was good news for a change. The entry on that date, July 25, stated that "our Flie boate, and the rest of our planters, arrived, all safe at Hatoraske." Somehow, Edward Spicer, the flyboat captain, who had never been to Virginia, had traced Ferdinando's route, successfully reaching his destination only days after the experienced mariner. The colonists transported by Spicer on the flyboat joined those already ashore, making ready their new homes in America, as Ferdinando waited impatiently at anchor off Hatorask.

There is no report of any Indians being seen during those first few days on the island. No doubt the apparent absence of Indians led to a false sense of security and a relaxing of any safety measures White may have ordered. The naive approach of these inexperienced settlers was illustrated by the actions of George Howe, one of White's twelve assistants, who less than a week after the arrival on Roanoke Island decided to go crabbing alone. Stripped almost naked, leaving his weapons on shore with his clothes and carrying only a forked stick, he was wading in the shallow waters some two miles from his fellow settlers when a group of Indians hidden in the reeds suddenly attacked the defenseless man. They promptly "gave him sixteene wounds with their arrowes: and after they had slaine him with their woodden swordes, beat his head in peeces, and fled over the water to the maine."

Two days later, White sent "Master Stafford" (undoubtedly the same Edward Stafford who had served as captain of one of Lane's companies, and the one who was manning the lookout station near Cape Hatteras [Croatoan] when Drake's fleet arrived) in a small boat to Croatoan with Manteo and twenty of the colonists. Croatoan was Manteo's birthplace, and members of his family still lived there. White hoped that he and Stafford could gather information about the fate of Grenville's men, and at the same time get some indication of the activities of Wanchese and the other Roanoac Indians who had survived the massacre at Dasamonquepeuc.

But even Manteo's Croatoans had grown wary of the men from England, for when the small group landed on the sound side back of Cape Hatteras, the Indians at first appeared ready to fight, then "perceaving us begin to marche with out shot towards them, they turned their backes, and fled."

Manteo, the world-traveler-returned, then called out to

them, and as soon as they heard his voice, the Indians returned "and threwe away their bowes, and arrowes, and some of them came unto us, embracing and entertaining us friendly." Remembering the high-handed actions of Grenville and Lane, the people of Manteo's birthplace begged the Englishmen "not to gather or spill any of their corne, for that they had but little." Stafford, probably using Manteo as an interpreter, assured them that "neither their corne, nor any other thing of theirs, should be diminished by any of us, and that our comming was onely to renew the olde love, that was betweene us, and them, at the first, and to live with them as brethren, and friendes." How quickly could sweet words and promises win over these native people, for the answer "seemed to please them well, wherefore they requested us to walke up to their Towne, who there feasted us after their manner."

Stafford and his men remained at Croatoan overnight, and the next day "had conference further with them, concerning the people of Secota, Aquascogoc, & Pomiock." They urged Manteo's people to serve as intermediaries, specifically, to transmit a message that if the natives aligned with the deceased Wingina "would accept our friendship, we would willingly receave them againe, and that all unfriendly dealings past on both partes, should be utterly forgiven, and forgotten."

The answer from the Croatoans was that they would "gladly doe the best they could, and within seven daies, bring the Weroances and chiefe Governours of those townes with them, to our Governour at Roanoak."

The Croatoans then told them, in some detail, of the fate of Grenville's party. The members of the detachment had conducted themselves in a careless manner, and some thirty of Wingina's men, from the towns of Secotan, Aquascogoc, and Dasamonquepeuc, had launched an attack under the pretense of friendship and killed one of the Englishmen. The survivors assembled in a single building, possibly the structure in the fort, but the Indians set it afire and the defenders were forced to flee, taking up "such weapons as came first to hand, and without order to runne foorth among the Savages, with whome they skirmished above an howre." The advantage was all on the side of the Indians, for they were fighting in the forest away from the protection of the houses and fort, yet the hour-long conflict ended in a draw—one Indian killed and one Englishman "shotte into the mouth with an arrowe, whereof he died."

The colonists finally retreated toward the shore "where their boate lay, with which they fled towards Hatorask," picking up on the way four of their company "comming from a creeke thereby, where they had bene to fetch Oysters." The survivors, the report concludes, then "landed on a little Island on the right hand of our entrance into the harbour of Hatorask, where they remained a while, but afterward departed, whither, as yet we knowe not."

Thus we have yet another chapter in the mystery of what happened to the settlers on Roanoke Island. Three men had been left there by Lane a year earlier; the body of one had subsequently been found by Grenville, the fate of the other two was unknown. Now, of the fifteen men Grenville had left on Roanoke Island, two had been killed in the skirmish with the Indians and the remaining thirteen apparently had gotten away safely in their boat, though some were wounded. Did they remain on the Outer Banks until they died of starvation or were killed by Wanchese and Wingina's followers? Did they set sail in their small boat in the hope that somehow, against all odds, they could cross the broad Atlantic and return home safely to England? Or did they, perhaps, join friendly natives elsewhere and gradually become absorbed into their tribe? No one knows.

Before Stafford's departure from Croatoan the Indians came to him with a special request. They pointed out that all Indians seemed to look alike to the average Englishman, for in the summer months they wore practically no clothing, and there was no appreciable difference in their coloration or mannerisms. As a result, the year before, Lane's men had mistaken several friendly Croatoans for Wingina's followers and launched an attack in which "divers of them were hurt." As proof, they took Stafford to see one man "which at that very instant laye lame, and had lien of that hurt ever since." The Croatoans said they knew Lane had attacked them by mistake, "wherefore they held us excused," but were deathly afraid the same thing might happen again. They proposed, therefore, "that there might be some token or badge given them of us, whereby we might know them to be our friendes, when we met them any where out of the Towne or Island." Unfortunately, if this proposal made sense to Stafford, he did no more than take it under advisement.

The Croatoans gave Stafford one final bit of intelligence, which he relayed to White back at Roanoke Island. George Howe had been "slaine by the remnant of Winginoes men, dwelling then at Dasamonqueponke, with whom Winchese kept companie." The colonists' reaction to this information, combined with their failure to heed the suggestion of the Croatoans that they be provided with some sort of identifying "token or badge," produced dire results.

Governor White waited impatiently for the Croatoan messengers to bring some word as promised from the weroances of Secotan, Aquascogoc, and Dasamonquepeuc in response to his proposal that they let bygones be bygones and resume friendly relations. After a full week, with "no tidings of them heard," the governor and his assistants made a fateful decision: they would make clear to Wanchese and the other Roanoacs that such action as the slaying of Howe would not be tolerated.

The method chosen to teach this lesson to the "savages" seems so out of keeping with White's overall approach to successful colonization that it must be assumed in this instance the views of some of his more militant assistants prevailed. It was almost as though they had just finished reading Lane's account of his troubles with Wingina and decided to take a page from the soldier's journal. The plan adopted was to send Captain Stafford and twenty-four men, with Manteo serving as guide, across the sound under cover of darkness to launch a surprise predawn attack on the mainland Indian town of Dasamonquepeuc.

In all respects but one this second Dasamonquepeuc raid was a highly successful undertaking. Stafford reported that he and his men "landed neere the dwelling place of our enemies, and very secretly conveyed our selves through the woods, to that side where we had their houses betweene us and the water." Several Indians, early risers, were seated around a fire when Stafford launched his attack. The Indians were taken completely by surprise, and in utter confusion "the miserable soules . . . fledde into a place of thicke reedes, growing fast by." Stafford's men, in close pursuit, "shotte one of them through the bodie with a bullet" and were closing in on the others when one of the natives, appealing for mercy, suddenly shouted Captain Stafford's name. At almost the same time it became clear that one of the Indians was carrying a child in a back sling. This was a woman, not a warrior.

Only then did the truth become apparent. These were not Roanoacs, the followers of Wingina. Rather, these were Croatoans, Manteo's people, come from their home far across the sound to gather up the surplus corn left by Wanchese and the others who had long since fled Dasamonquepeuc after killing Howe.

The always faithful Manteo, Governor White's one remaining tie with the native Americans, had unwittingly participated in a fatal attack on his own people.

CHAPTER 14

Virginia Dare

Manteo reacted immediately to Governor White's misguided attack on the Croatoans at Dasamonquepeuc. He was "grieved" and obviously angry. His anger, however, was directed not at the colonists but at his own people, for "he imputed their harme to their owne follie, saying to them, that if their Weroans had kept their promise in comming to the Governour, at the day appointed, they had not knowen that mischance."

Four days later, on August 13, the colonists showed their appreciation. On that date, it was recorded, "our Savage Manteo, by the commandement of Sir Walter Ralegh, was christened in Roanoak, and called Lord therof, and of Dasamongueponke, in reward of his faithfull service."

It had taken more than three years, but the men of England had at last established their claim to a little piece of the North American continent, much as the Spanish conquistadors had in the Caribbean and Central and South America nearly a century earlier. They had murdered the king of the country, driven his followers from their native land, and installed their own loyal vassal as "Lord" of the conquered territory. They had hardly followed the advice of Hakluyt, and the expressed intent of Governor White, to "renew the olde love" with the native people and "live with them as brethren, and friendes."

August 18 must have been an especially happy day for the little band of colonist families on Roanoke Island, for on that day Eleanor White Dare gave birth to a daughter. Six days later, on Sunday, the newborn child was christened "Virginia," in honor of being "the first Christian borne in Virginia." Thus, in rapid sequence, Manteo had become the first North American Indian admitted to the Church of England, and Virginia Dare had become both the first child born of English parents in America and the first christened in the new land.

Meanwhile, Simon Ferdinando, who had refused to sail on up the coast to Chesapeake Bay in July because it was so late in the season, had ridden at anchor off the Outer Banks with his little fleet for more than a month while the tedious work of transporting the colonists and their gear to the temporary Cittie of Ralegh on Roanoke Island was undertaken. Throughout that month the White journal makes not a single mention of Ferdinando, and one wonders, if the White version of the mariner's earlier actions is to be believed, why Ferdinando didn't just weigh anchor and take off in pursuit of prizes.

As the time approached for the vessels to return to England, the colonists were faced with another concern. There was general agreement throughout the settlement that at least one and preferably two of the governor's assistants should return home with Ferdinando to secure supplies needed for "the good and happie planting" of the colony. But the matter of determining which two of the assistants should make the voyage was not as simple as it might appear, for it developed that none of them wanted to go. At one point, "by much perswading of the Governour," Christopher Cooper, apparently a single man, agreed to undertake the assignment. A day later, however, "through the perswasion of divers of his familiar friendes, he changed his minde, so that now the matter stoode as at the first."

Even as these discussions were taking place on shore,

Ferdinando was facing his own problems. He awoke one morning to find that the wind, so long content to blow gently from the southwest, was now coming furiously from the northeast. This was a summer northeaster of the kind still typical along the Outer Banks, and as the wind increased to gale force, the once gentle waves, now massive ocean rollers, were topped with frothing white caps as far out as one could see from shore. Ferdinando "was forced to cut his cables, and put to Sea."

If any of the colonists were concerned that Ferdinando might use the storm as an excuse to abandon the settlement, they gave no indication of it, for they all seemed obsessed with a single question: Who among them should return to England? On August 22, the day after the northeaster had forced Ferdinando to put to sea, these discussions took quite a different tack. This time "the whole companie, both of the Assistants, and planters, came to the Governour, and with one voice requested him to returne himselfe into England, for the better and sooner obtaining of supplies, and other necessaries for them."

White faced a quandary. He knew, possibly better than any of them, how important it was for at least one responsible member of the colony to return home for the needed supplies. None could say he had not done his best to convince the individual assistants, one after another, to make the voyage, yet not a single man had agreed to leave. Now they, in turn, were calling on him to carry out the undertaking. But there were so many reasons why he should remain with his planters in Virginia. There seemed to be no question that Roanoke Island was only a temporary base and that as soon as possible his colony should relocate, either to Chesapeake Bay as originally planned or to some fertile and protected site on the mainland. He was the one responsible for deciding when and where they should move; and he was the one who should be there to lead the little band of men, women, and children when the time came for such an exodus.

There were still other concerns, not the least of which was how it would appear back in England, to Raleigh and the backers of the colony and even casual observers, if he, the governor, abandoned his settlers and returned home. White expressed concern that he might be discredited for "leaving the action" and that some would assume he had undertaken the American venture in the first place for political reasons only, leading so many of his fellow Englishmen "into a Countrey, in which he never meant to stay himselfe."

Finally, there were the personal concerns. He would have to leave behind on Roanoke Island not only his daughter but his newborn granddaughter as well. And what about his paints and brushes and the other supplies needed for completing his drawings of America, and even the drawings themselves? Already, while he was away from the settlement on a brief excursion, someone had ransacked his personal belongings. He was concerned that if the colonists moved before his return, "his stuffe and goods, might be both spoiled, and most of it pilfered away in the carriage," leaving him "utterly unfurnished" when he returned to Virginia. No, White said, under no circumstances would he be the one to leave.

If Governor White had shown himself to be dogged in his determination, so also did his fellow colonists. To many of them he seemed their only hope for securing proper relief supplies and signing on additional planters. Just one day after he had turned down their initial request they came to him again and presented their case with even more persuasion. This time "not onely the Assistants, but divers others, as well women, as men, beganne to renewe their requests," begging their leader to return in Ferdinando's fleet "for the supplie, and dispatch of all such thinges, as there were to be done." This time, also, they put it all down in writing, a legal and binding document, "under all their handes, and seales."

Dated "the five and twentieth of August," just one day

after the baptism of Virginia Dare, it read in part as follows:

> May it please you, her Majesties Subjects of England, wee your friendes and Countrey men, the planters in Virginia, doe by these presents let you, and every of you to understande, that for the present and speedie supplie of certaine our knowen, and apparent lackes, and needes, most requisite and necessarie for the good and happie planting of us, or any other in this lande of Virginia, wee all of one minde, and consent, have most earnestly intreated, and uncessantly requested John White, Governour of the planters in Virginia, to passe into England, for the better and more assured helpe, and setting forward of the foresayde supplies.

All of White's concerns seemed covered. The document pointed out that, "not once, but often," he had refused their request to make the voyage and that he had finally and reluctantly agreed "for our sakes, and for the honour, and maintenance of the action" to leave "his government, and all his goods among us, and himselfe in all our behalfes to passe into Englande."

In addition, the settlers drew up and signed a bond "for the safe preserving of all his goods for him at his returne to Virginia." It provided that "if any part thereof were spoiled, or lost, they would see it restored to him, or his Assignes, whensoever the same should be missed, and demanded."

There was little time for White to reflect on these entreatments and inducements when they were presented to him. The northeaster had abated, and with the Outer Banks once again bathed in bright sunlight and caressed by the soft breezes that invariably are nature's rewards for enduring such storms, Ferdinando had in fact returned. His vessels were at anchor off the coast again, but he had sent word ashore that he was departing for the Atlantic voyage on the next tide. White made no mention of those last few hours on Roanoke Island, but it is easy to picture the scene as he rushed to gather up the necessities for the long voyage. He had to leave last-minute instructions with his assistants; carefully pack the precious letters laboriously written by members of the colony for delivery to loved ones back home; endure the sad and poignant parting with his daughter, Eleanor; and take a final peek at the tiny baby, Virginia Dare. With all this accomplished at last, Governor White bade farewell to his assistants, his planters, and his family and boarded a small boat for the passage across the sound and through the inlet to Ferdinando's fleet riding at anchor offshore. White, a deeply religious man, must have said a final, silent prayer as the low profile of Roanoke gradually faded from his view.

White has given us no indication as to whom he left in charge of the little band of colonists who remained on Roanoke Island. The number of assistants had been reduced to no more than ten—for George Howe was dead, and Ferdinando was returning to England—and the names of three others are not included in the list of those left behind, leading to speculation that they never left England.

Information is lacking, as well, with regard to the experience and background of the various assistants, and even their ages. Only two were accompanied by their families: Ananias Dare, father of Virginia Dare, and Dyonis Harvie, whose wife Margery had also given birth to a child before White's departure, though there is no indication of whether this second offspring of English parentage was a boy or a girl. The other assistants who remained were Christopher Cooper, Roger Bailie, John Sampson, Thomas Stevens, and Roger Pratt. Was one of these made acting governor of the Cittie of Ralegh in Virginea? We likely will never know.

There is confusion even as to the number of colonists who remained, even though Hakluyt published at the end of White's narrative the names of "all the men, women and Children, which safely arrived in Virginia, and remained to inhabite there." Listed are 91 men, 17 women, 9 "Boyes and Children," and 2 "Children born in Virginia"—a total of 119. The trouble with the list is that it includes the names of White, Howe, and Ferdinando, each of whom departed in one way or another, and the names of the two Indians, Manteo and Towaye, "that were in Englande and returned home into Virginia with them." There has been resultant disagreement and confusion among historians concerning the size of the colony, with the figure generally ranging from 110 to 119, not counting the Indians. Lefler and Newsome played it safe, putting the number at "about 110." Simple arithmetic—subtracting the names of White, Howe, and Ferdinando from the 119 names listed—produces the figure used here of 116.

Neither did White pass on any information about the instructions he undoubtedly left concerning what the colonists should do and where they should go in his absence. He did say that he arranged a way for them to let him know where they had gone if they decided to leave Roanoke Island before his return from England—the name of their new location, carved on a conspicuous tree or post. And if the move had to be made because of an attack by Indians or Spaniards or other danger, they "should carve over the letters or name" a distress signal in the form of a Maltese cross. But that was all. Except, of course, that Manteo remained behind this time, as befitting the newly ordained Lord of Roanoke and Dasamonquepeuc.

White must have had second thoughts about agreeing to return to England even before he had lost sight of the Carolina coast. He sailed on the flyboat, rather than on Ferdinando's flagship, *Lyon*, quite possibly because of the animosity between him and the mariner. As the flyboat crewmen struggled to raise the anchor off Hatorask, there occurred one of those bizarre accidents that have always plagued men of the sea. Twelve of the seamen were crowded together on the forecastle, straining in unison against the wooden bars that turned the capstan. This was the manual process employed to bring aboard the anchor and chain, and it called for a back-breaking effort on the part of each man. But, suddenly, one of the bars broke. Immediately, the dead weight of the anchor and chain falling down again toward the ocean floor caused the capstan to reverse. Like a wound-up rubber-band motor let loose, the remaining capstan bars flailed the poor seamen with tremendous force. All twelve were "throwen from the Capestone," several receiving injuries so severe that they "never recovered it." Those still able to function tried "againe to weigh their anker, but being so weakened with the first fling, they were not able to weigh it, but were throwen downe, and hurt the seconde time." That was enough for Captain Edward Spicer. He ordered the cable cut so they could get underway.

The flyboat was a sizable vessel of some 100 tons, but at the time of the departure from the Outer Banks she carried a relatively small crew of only fifteen men, barely enough to sail her properly in heavy weather. The Atlantic crossing must have been a frightful experience for all on board, for when they finally reached Flores in the Azores some three weeks later, only five of the seamen were fit for duty. Since the flyboat was still in consort with *Lyon*, it would have seemed logical for Ferdinando to provide replacements from his flagship. But many of the crewmen of both vessels had come down with some sort of sickness, and since Ferdinando planned to remain in the vicinity of the Azores in the hope of taking a prize or two, he probably felt that he needed every man he could muster. Shorthanded as he was, Spicer then decided it was best for him to press on toward England—but the elements seemed bent on teaming up against him.

White's journal provides hints of the problems they encountered. "Having had sometimes scarce, and variable windes, our fresh water also by leaking almost consumed," he said, "there arose a storme at Northeast, which for 6. dayes ceased not to blowe so exceeding, that we were driven further in those 6. then wee could recover in thirteene daies." By that time they were further from England than they had been when they left Flores, but things got even worse. "Others of our saylers began to fall very sicke," White said, "and two of them dyed." On top of all that, the weather continued so bad that "our Master sometimes in foure daies together could see neither Sunne nor starre, and all the beverage we could make, with stinking water, dreggs of beere, and lees of wine which remained," amounted to a total of only three gallons for everyone on board. At that time, White, veteran of three voyages to Virginia, survivor of Indian attacks and of near-starvation, reached the point where he "expected nothing but by famyne to perish at Sea."

Then, quite unexpectedly, in mid-October, some seven weeks after the departure from Virginia, the men aboard the flyboat sighted land. They had reached western Ireland, and help was at hand: other vessels riding there at anchor provided them with emergency rations—"fresh water, wyne, and other fresh meate." Two days later, Governor White and Captain Spicer went ashore to the nearby town of Dingle where they planned to "take order of the new victualling of our Flye boate for England, and for reliefe of our sicke and hurt men." For some of the members of the crew, however, it was too late. Within four days "the boatswane, the steward, and the boatswanes mate dyed aboord the flyeboate," and shortly afterward three more men became so ill that they had to be taken ashore. White had had enough of the flyboat. Carrying letters from his colonists, anxious to report to Raleigh and then get about the task of assembling supplies for his return to Virginia, he left Dingle on November 1 as a passenger on "a ship called the *Monkie*," which reached Marazion, in Cornwall, on the fifth of the month.

Had White been a vindictive man he might have taken pleasure from the report he heard out of Portsmouth concerning the arrival there, three weeks earlier, of Simon Ferdinando and his *Lyon*. Not only had Ferdinando failed totally in his privateering efforts, but he arrived off Portsmouth with his crew "in such weaknesse by sicknes, and death of their cheefest men, that they were scarse able to bring their ship into the harbour, but were forced to let fall anker without, which they could not way againe, but might all have perished there, if a small barke by great hap had not come to them to helpe them."

In the annals of the Raleigh colonization attempts this is the last heard of Simon Ferdinando, described by Quinn as "a violent, quarrelsome, and unattractive though able man." However, he later served with distinction in the great naval war with Spain.

John White, of course, would remain a part of the Roanoke story. He had a daughter and granddaughter there, and others who depended on him. Moreover, he was still governor of the "Cittie of Ralegh in Virginea," and he had much to do before returning to America.

CHAPTER 15

The Spanish Armada

If ever a person's timing was out of rhythm with events of the day then surely John White's was when he returned to England in the fall of 1587 to line up relief supplies and additional colonists for his settlement on Roanoke Island.

In mid-October, at the very time when he and the other survivors of accident and illness aboard Spicer's flyboat were rejoicing at having finally sighted the friendly shores of Ireland, word was circulating throughout the British Isles of the action of the Privy Council just one week earlier, ordering a stay of all English shipping. King Philip of Spain—who had reigned briefly as joint sovereign of England by virtue of his four-year marriage (1554–58) to Queen Mary I—was assembling the mightiest seaborne force ever put together for a massive attack on Elizabeth's England, and all British shipping was needed for defense against the Spanish Armada.

In retrospect it is ironic that the attempts by Raleigh and his associates to establish a North American colony may have contributed to Philip's decision to have it out, once and for all, with England. Ever since Columbus established the initial claim in 1492, America had been Spain's private domain, a veritable lode of treasure, a colonial empire unmatched in history. French efforts to break the Spanish hold—in Canada, and at Charlesfort and Fort

Caroline—had ended in total failure. Minor intrusions by such as England's Sir John Hawkins and Sir Humphrey Gilbert were nothing more than temporary irritations. But Raleigh's colonizing claim to much of the North American continent and Sir Francis Drake's bold and successful raids at the heart of Spain's American colonies were something else again. King Philip reasoned, and rightly so, that England had to be stopped, and soon. How better to cut off the threat than to assemble a flotilla so powerful as to make inevitable the conquering of Elizabeth's naval forces, and even England itself?

Those loyal supporters of the queen, Sir Walter Raleigh and Sir Richard Grenville, knights of the realm and men of the sea, appeared fully supportive of the Privy Council's stay of shipping. Along with Drake, Hawkins, and others they began making plans to ready their own vessels and assemble others for the ultimate defense of Britain against the forces of Spain.

Some six weeks later, on November 20, when Governor White was finally able to make a full report in person on the events of the preceding summer, Raleigh's allegiance to the crown must have been truly tested. The very life of his country was threatened by Philip. But the lives of his planters and the success of his efforts to colonize Virginia were in peril also. His decision was not long in coming; he no doubt rationalized that the continued harassment of Spain in the West Indies and the maintenance of a permanent English base in his Virginia were as important to the defense of England as any action he could take at home.

Despite the formal stay on shipping, he called on Grenville to assemble a fleet of at least half a dozen vessels for an expedition to leave England as soon as possible with dual objectives: relief for the Cittie of Ralegh and further incursions in the West Indies. It soon became apparent, however, that Grenville could not possibly assemble his fleet until late winter at the earliest. Yet it seemed prudent to arrange for Governor White to return to Virginia at the earliest possible time. Accordingly, Raleigh "appointed a pinnesse to be sent thither with all such necessaries as he understood they stood in neede of." He even wrote letters to some of the leaders among the colonists "wherein among other matters he comforted them with promise, that with all convenient speede he would prepare a good supply of shipping and men with sufficience of all thinges needefull, which he intended, God willing, should be with them the Sommer following." But the pinnace never sailed, possibly, as historian Quinn speculates, because of the fear "that a small unescorted vessel was unlikely to survive Spanish attacks on the southern route, while a winter crossing by the more difficult northern route was even more hazardous."

Disappointed as Governor White must have been at this turn of events, he nonetheless busied himself recruiting additional colonists and securing supplies and equipment in anticipation of Grenville's much more ambitious venture scheduled for the following spring. He was not the only one hard at work, for in something like four months, record time for such preparations, Grenville was ready for the voyage. The last week in March his fleet, numbering seven or eight vessels, was loaded and at anchor in the harbor at Bideford, "staying but for a faire wind to put to Sea."

Even as Grenville waited aboard his flagship, however, an urgent communication from the Privy Council was delivered to him. There were new and startling reports of the "invincible fleetes" being assembled by the king of Spain "joyned with the power of the Pope for the invading of England." As a result, once again, ships of war "in any haven in England were stayed for service at home," and Grenville "was personally commanded not to depart out of Cornewall." The order, clear and unequivocal, and dated March 31, 1588, instructed Grenville to join Sir Francis Drake with "suche shippes as were of greatest burthen and fyttest for service." But since Grenville's flotilla included certain smaller craft not suited for defense against the Spanish Armada, he was authorized, if Drake agreed, to "dyspose of and employ" them in his intended expedition to America.

This must have gladdened the heart of Governor White, for it specifically authorized Drake to release such vessels as he considered unsuitable for the defense effort and gave permission for them to be sent to Virginia for relief of Raleigh's colony. The two small craft selected were the 30-ton bark *Brave* and the 25-ton pinnace *Roe*. Accompanying White were fifteen "planters and all their provision, with certaine reliefe for those that wintered" on Roanoke Island. It had taken longer than he had expected or hoped, but with his mission to England accomplished, the governor was finally en route back to his new home across the sea.

If the selection of vessels for this undertaking left something to be desired, imagine White's concern when he recognized the caliber of the individuals assigned to man them. Obviously, the best and most qualified of Grenville's captains and officers had to be kept aboard the larger warships in preparation for the expected confrontation with Philip's Armada. Left to command the two-vessel expedition bound for Virginia was Captain Arthur Facy, a veteran of Grenville's 1586 voyage, but a man apparently more interested in plunder than in planting. The pilot was a Spaniard, Pedro Diaz, captured on an earlier voyage and pressed into British service. These men knew their way to Virginia, but seemed totally lacking in motivation for reaching that destination.

Having weathered the shock of Ferdinando's decision to dump his settlers on Roanoke Island, his concern over the mistaken attack on the friendly Croatoans at Dasamonquepeuc, and finally his harrowing experience aboard Spicer's flyboat on the return voyage, White must have felt that he was prepared for any adversity. But in his wildest and most chilling nightmares he could not have dreamed of what was about to happen to him and the new colonists aboard *Brave*.

The two vessels carrying White and his fifteen planters set sail for Virginia on April 22, 1588, and the following day Facy began his privateering activities while the coast of England was still in sight. His little bark, *Brave*, and the even smaller pinnace, *Roe*, gave chase to four ships, forcing them "to come to anker by us in a small bay at the lands end." This initial success proved unrewarding, however, for the ships carried nothing of value, and after impressing three men to add to his own crew Facy released the captured vessels and put to sea again under cover of darkness.

The following day two more vessels were encountered, and again Facy gave chase. "These we borded also," White reported in his journal, "& tooke from them whatsoever we could find worth the taking." For the next week Facy's little flotilla skirted the English coast, on one occasion exchanging gunfire at close range with a vessel mistakenly thought at first to be an Englishman, and on another chasing a 200-ton Spanish ship so close to the coast of Spain that Facy, "fearing eyther change of wind or to be calmed gave over the fight and put off to Sea againe."

On May 3 *Brave* and *Roe* sighted what was described as "another tal ship" and took off in pursuit of what appeared to be a rich prize. As darkness fell, those on board *Brave* lost sight of the consort, *Roe*, as well as the other ship, and at dawn the following morning both had disappeared. Facy then set a course for the island of Madeira, "hoping there to find our pinnesse abiding for us."

Eleven days after setting sail from England, Facy's bark was just then beginning its intended voyage to Virginia. But whereas the little pinnace, *Roe*, appeared well equipped for privateering, the larger *Brave* was poorly suited for such activity, or even for its own defense. She was "so bad of sayle," White said, "that we could neither take nor leve, but were rather to be taken or left of every ship we met." Two days after losing sight of the pinnace, *Brave* became engaged in just the sort of encounter White had feared—as the hunted rather than the hunter.

"We spake with a man of warre of Rochel of 60 tons, very wel manned & bravely appointed," White said, and "parted frindly in outward shew . . . but nevertheles we suspected yt which followed." The problem was that "this Rocheller," as White described the French warship, had "taken perfect view of our ship, men, & ordinance," and having sized up *Brave* as being an easy target, "towards evening fell on sterne of us and assone as it was darke left us, and returned to his consort which was a tal ship of 100 tonne lying then on hull to weather of us."

The following morning, May 6, the two vessels were so close to *Brave* that there was no chance of escape, and Facy prepared his 30-ton bark for combat with the two larger vessels. White described the initial encounter: "The same day about 2 of the clocke in the afternoone they were come with us. We hayled them, but them would not answere. We . . . gave them one whole side: with one of our great shot their Master gonners shoolder was stroken away, and our Master gonner with a smal bullet was shot into the head. Being by this time grappled and aboord each of other the fight continued without ceasing one houre and a halfe." It was a bloody battle, with many casualties on both sides. Twenty-three "of the chiefest men" on both sides "were hurt & slaine," some with as many as "10 or 12 woundes." White himself "was wounded twice in the head, once with a sword, and another time with a pike, and hurt also in the side of the buttoke with a shot."

The result was inevitable. "Having spent all the powder in our flaskes and charges which we had present for our defence," White recorded, "they cut downe our netting and entred so many of their men as could stand upon our poope and forecastle, from whence they playd extreemely upon us with their shot." Outnumbered, defenseless, and cornered like animals in a slaughterhouse, Facy and his men surrendered. But this was not the end, for the members of the boarding party, "knowing so many of their best men to be hurt and in danger of present death, began to grow into a new furie, in which they would have put us to the sword had not their Captaine charged them, and persuaded them to the contrary."

Having lost the battle with the French man-of-war, and now prisoners on their own ship, White and his planters, as well as *Brave's* crewmen, could only stand by and watch as the captors looted their vessel of everything worth taking, including personal belongings and the supplies intended for Virginia. This continued until the afternoon of the following day, "at which time by over greedy lading both their owne boate and ours, they sunke the one and split the other by the ships side."

When at last the enemy vessels took their leave, the few men still able to perform their duties aboard the little bark set about "mending our sailes, tacklings, and such other things as were spilled in our fight." White's disappointment showed all too clearly as he reported that "we were of force constrained to break of our voyage intended for the reliefe of our Colony left the yere before in Virginia, and the same night to set our course for England."

Undermanned and defenseless, *Brave* made slow passage as Facy kept his small vessel well at sea, "fearing to meete with any more men of warre, for that we had no maner of weapons left us." It was two weeks before they sighted "the Northside of Cornewal at the lands end," and on May 22 they finally "put over the barre, and the same day landed at Biddeford." The final entry in White's journal of the 1588 expedition was a notation that the little pinnace *Roe* returned "home into Cornwall within fewe weekes after our arrival, without performing our intended voyage for the reliefe of the planters in Virginia, which thereby were not a little distressed."

Even then Spain's mighty Armada was assembled at Lisbon for the attack on England. One of the greatest naval battles in recorded history was at hand, and any thought of attempting another voyage to Virginia that summer of 1588 was of necessity abandoned.

The Spanish Armada consisted of some 130 ships manned by an estimated eight thousand seamen, and carrying upwards of nineteen thousand armed soldiers especially trained for the planned landing on English soil. Even the ships were formidable, mostly galleons, heavily armed for action at close quarters.

By comparison the English fleet was a mixed collection of craft, large and small, nearly 200 in all, carrying an estimated sixteen thousand men, the great majority experienced sailors. The most obvious difference in the makeup of the two fleets was that the Spanish vessels in almost all instances were slow and cumbersome, while those assembled for the defense of England were smaller but faster and more maneuverable.

The strategy developed so carefully by King Philip and his naval and military experts would have been apparent to any knowledgeable observer as the mighty Armada approached the English coast off Cornwall on July 19. These massive vessels were to remain in tight formation. Only those on the perimeter were to be exposed to direct contact with the enemy. The fleet moved forward relentlessly, bunched together in the manner of a rugby-football scrum.

The English fleet, having assembled at Portsmouth, was almost trapped before escaping into the Channel. Once in the open sea the advantage was with the English, for their faster, more maneuverable ships and longer-range guns allowed them to fire on the Spanish galleons without being hit by return fire. In the first three engagements, however, they were unable to do appreciable damage, and the Armada anchored intact on July 27 in the French harbor of Calais. This error in judgment was soon seized upon by the English, commanded by such brilliant tacticians as Drake and Hawkins.

On the night of July 28 the immobile Spanish Armada was attacked with fireships. Sailors on the tightly grouped Spanish vessels panicked, cut their anchor lines, and fled the harbor in disarray. The following day off Gravelines the English pressed their advantage, devastating the disorganized Armada. A violent storm enabled the Spanish to escape, but many of the cumbersome galleons were wrecked. More still were lost as the once mighty fleet sailed on around Scotland and Ireland. When the storm and the battle had ended, fewer than eighty ships returned safely to Spain.

This was a joyous day for England. Britannia was to rule the seas of the world for centuries thereafter. Spain's domination of America was broken also. But here and there, as the victory was celebrated, surely certain individuals paused to reflect on the fate of Raleigh's colony, abandoned on Roanoke Island in faraway Virginia.

CHAPTER 16

White Returns

For something like a year and a half following the defeat of the Spanish Armada in August, 1588, there seems to have been no effort to send relief to the colonists on Roanoke Island, certainly at least no relief that could have produced meaningful results. There was talk, and unquestionably a lot of planning, and even the drawing up of formal documents intended to involve additional backers in the project; but throughout the fall of 1588 and all of 1589 no ships sailed for Virginia. Modern historians are at a loss to explain why no such effort was made.

Possibly it was because Raleigh had other things on his mind. Always interested in a wide variety of activities, ranging from the compounding of medical formulas and the study of philosophy to the use of mathematics as an aid to navigation, he was having personal problems as well. A favorite of the spinster queen and captain of her personal guard, Raleigh was involved in an affair with one of her handmaidens which culminated in a secret marriage. And he seemed to be giving more and more of his attention to other colonial ventures, such as the one that resulted a few years later in his own voyage to Guiana. It seems clear that his interest in the faltering Virginia venture had waned.

Others, however, were as concerned as ever about the

fate of the settlers on Roanoke Island and still confident over the prospects for Virginia colonization. One of those whose interest remained high was Richard Hakluyt, and early in 1589 he became officially associated with the Cittie of Ralegh. Under date of March 7, 1589, Raleigh signed an agreement with nineteen "Gentlemen, and Merchants of London," including Hakluyt, and with Governor White and the assistants of the Cittie of Ralegh, giving them broad rights to proceed with the undertaking. They were to have, forever, "free trade, and traffique for all manner of Marchandise, or commodities" to and from all that part of America "called Asamacomock, alias Wingandacoia, alias Virginia." (The new name, Asamacomock, or Ossomocomuck, had by that time been recognized as the one used by the native people for the area Raleigh's early explorers had mistakenly referred to as Wingandacon.)

This expanded group of gentlemen, merchants, and assistants now numbered nearly thirty. The list included at least seven who had been left on Roanoke Island, plus White, Hakluyt, and William Sanderson. As the manager of Raleigh's business affairs, Sanderson was so closely associated with him that he was to claim later that on several occasions Sir Walter owed him "more then a hundred Thousand poundes starling." They were expected, upon sealing the agreement, to "adventure divers & sundry sums of money, marchandises, shiping, munition, victual, and other commodities, into the said forraine and remote country." This sixteenth-century agreement bears a striking resemblance to some of the modern business deals that involve seemingly astronomical sums of money but call for the actual transfers of only infinitesimal amounts. Raleigh sealed the bargain with a good-faith cash binder of "one hundred pounds of lawful money of England."

What were these nineteen gentlemen and merchants actually planning at the time the agreement took effect in the early spring of 1589? Had they already secured a ship or ships for the relief of the settlers? Was White waiting at dockside with additional recruits for the Roanoke Island colony? Why did they wait a full year longer before arranging for the governor of the planters in Virginia to return to his American settlement? No one seems to have come up with any of the answers to these questions.

It was March, 1590, a full two years and seven months after his August, 1587, departure from Roanoke Island, before White set sail on the journey that would eventually return him to his colony. But White, the governor of the Virginia plantation, seems to have been little more than a passenger on one of a small flotilla of vessels belonging to a company of London merchants headed by John Watts, who had received official "letters of reprisal" for operations against Spanish shipping. In short, this was a privateering venture first, with relief of the Virginia settlers at best a secondary objective.

The Watts fleet consisted of three small vessels, headed by *Hopewell*, of which Abraham Cooke was captain and Robert Hutton, the master. Supporting the flagship was *Little John*, the "vice-admiral," commanded by Captain Christopher Newport; and *John Evangelist*, a pinnace, with William Lane as captain. A fourth vessel, owned by William Sanderson, was scheduled to make the voyage with them. This was *Moonlight*, with a familiar figure in the Virginia voyages, Edward Spicer, as captain. But *Moonlight* was left behind when the other three sailed from Plymouth on March 20. This could well have been deliberate, for *Moonlight*'s mission had more to do with relieving White's colonists than raiding Spanish treasure ships.

It was customary on voyages of this sort to carry small boats on the decks of the larger ships, not only for emergencies at sea but also for landings on alien coasts and explorations of the rivers and bays they visited. But the tenders for this expedition, two small shallops, were being towed when the vessels left Plymouth, and five days later, "by the Boatswaines negligence," both were sunk.

Otherwise it was a relatively uneventful crossing. On

April 1 two ship's boats, replacements for the lost shallops, were secured from "two great shippes of London" at Santa Cruz. On April 5, in the Canaries, they chased and captured a double flyboat, killing three members of the crew. Two days later they made a landing on Grand Canary to take on water, and on April 9 the three vessels set sail for the long voyage to the West Indies.

As often happened, the first landfall in the Caribbean was the island of Dominica, one of the Leeward Islands, located between Martinique and Guadeloupe, approximately midway down the long sweeping arc of islands and islets stretching from Puerto Rico to the South American mainland. The crossing had taken only twenty-three days, exceptionally good time, and the prospects were further brightened when large numbers of friendly "Salvages," remnants of the native Carib Indians, "came aboord our ships in their Canowes, and did traffique with us."

At Dominica, while the men rested and took on fresh food and water, plans were made for the raids against Spanish shipping. *Little John*, the vice-admiral, was to remain in the area for a few days, "playing off and on about Dominica, hoping to take some Spaniard outwardes bound to the Indies." *Hopewell* and *John Evangelist* would sail on toward Puerto Rico and Hispaniola, with a rendezvous set for some three weeks later on the southern coast of Hispaniola.

Once again White is the diarist; his account of the ensuing activities is the only detailed record available. Though he must have fretted over the delays resulting from the privateering activities when at last he was so close to his colony, at no time in his narrative does he complain. In fact, he seems almost to have relished being a part of such an operation, though it dragged on for months.

On the voyage from Dominica to Puerto Rico the two vessels sighted St. Kitts, then landed on one of the Virgin Islands, where they killed "an incredible number of foules." The two ships finally separated as they approached Puerto Rico; *Hopewell* sailed along the north shore and the little pinnace, *John Evangelist*, skirted the island's southern side. Not until May 7, after *Hopewell*'s crew had landed on the northwest end of Puerto Rico for fresh water, did the privateering begin to pay off, for that night *Hopewell* "tooke a Frigate of tenne Tunne . . . laden with hides and ginger."

On May 13 they made a landing on the island of Mona, midway between Puerto Rico and Haiti, "whereon were 10 or 12 houses inhabited of the Spaniards." The English privateers burned the houses "and tooke from them a Pinnesse, which they had drawen a ground and sunke, and carried all her sayles, mastes, and rudders into the woods" in an attempt to hide it from the Englishmen. The Spanish survivors were chased all over the island, but they hid "in caves, hollow rockes, and bushes, so that we could not find them." With this sporting activity at an end, *Hopewell* sailed on westward and was rejoined at the island of Saona, "lying on the Southside of Hispaniola neere the East end," by *Little John*, after an unsuccessful three weeks of hunting Spanish vessels. Shortly thereafter, at Cape Tiburon on the south side of Hispaniola, *John Evangelist* joined up with the other vessels, and Captain William Lane reported a harrowing experience in which the pinnace was attacked by a Spanish galley carrying some four hundred men.

Cape Tiburon had been selected with care as the base of operations for the little privateering fleet, for it was considered an ideal spot from which to intercept the Spanish treasure ships. It was three weeks after their rendezvous there, however, before the three vessels, now supported by the little frigate captured at Puerto Rico, were able to log their first successful action. Even that one must have been disappointing, for the vessel they captured was only "a smal Spanish frigat" with three men aboard and no cargo. The three, it developed, had just recently escaped from a Spanish prison at Santo Domingo and stolen the vessel.

But their leader, Anton Martin, a pilot and native of the Canary Islands, informed them that a large Spanish ship was even then taking on cargo at an isolated bay nearby.

Lane's pinnace, *John Evangelist*, with the little captured frigate as a consort, was selected for a quick, surprise attack on the Spanish ship, probably under cover of darkness. It was a week before the frigate returned with news that the expedition had been a total success and that *John Evangelist* "had taken the shippe, with many passengers and Negroes in the same." But there was disappointing news as well, for little of value had been found on the large vessel, since a "Frenchman of warre had taken and spoyled her" only a few days earlier.

By July 2 the little privateering fleet had taken on the appearance of a more formidable squadron. *John Evangelist* had returned to the rendezvous with a prize crew on board the captured ship, *Trinidad*, and on that date, Captain Edward Spicer in *Moonlight*, accompanied by a pinnace, the *Conclude*, joined forces with *Hopewell* and the others. Thus, briefly at least, the flotilla consisted of eight vessels: *Hopewell*, *Little John*, *John Evangelist*, *Moonlight*, *Conclude*, the prize ship *Trinidad*, and the two captured frigates. That very afternoon for the first time, a major Spanish treasure squadron was sighted—"14 saile all of Santo Domingo, to whom we presently gave chase." The Spanish ships almost immediately broke formation "and separating themselves scattered here and there." The English vessels in pursuit, according to White's account, "were forced to divide our selves and so made after them untill 12 of the clocke at night," at which point, "by reason of the darkenesse," they had "lost sight of ech other."

At dawn the following morning the privateers were so widely scattered that only *Moonlight* and the squadron leader, *Hopewell*, were still together, but they were in close pursuit of "the Vizadmirall of the Spanish fleete," a large vessel, richly laden, which they eventually captured.

Casualties on the English vessels were one dead and two wounded and on the Spanish side four dead and six wounded. As for the remaining six English vessels, the journal contains only this melancholy entry: "But what was become of our Viceadmirall, our Pinnesse, and Prize, and two Frigates, in all this time, we were ignorant."

The following day crewmen from *Hopewell* and *Moonlight* were engaged in "rifling, romaging and fitting the Prize to be sailed with us." With this activity accomplished and a prize crew aboard the captured ship, the three vessels sailed westward, at one point sighting Jamaica "on our larboord, keeping Cuba in sight on our starboard." The Isle of Pines was passed on July 8, and "the same day we gave chase to a Frigat, but at night we lost sight of her." A massive Spanish fleet of twenty-two vessels, "some of them of the burden of 300 and some 400 tunnes loaden with the Kings treasure from the maine, bound for Havana" was sighted by *Moonlight* on July 10, but the following day the winds died down and the vessels were becalmed. They remained that way, almost motionless on the smooth reflecting surface of the Caribbean Sea, for eleven days. During this period "the winde being scarse, and the weather exceeding hoat, we were much pestered with the Spaniards" who had been taken prisoner, and when at last the winds picked up, the captives were landed on the south side of Cuba.

Proceeding around Cuba's western end, then northward toward the Florida mainland, they sighted the upper islands of the Florida Keys and the Cape of Florida (just south of modern Miami) on July 23. For another week they sailed back and forth from Cuba to the mainland in search of Spanish ships; on one occasion they encountered but failed to capture "three small Pinnasses of S. John de Ullua bound for Havana, which were exceeding richly loaden"—though how White knew what the vessels carried is a mystery.

At last, on July 30, the decision was made to abandon the search for prizes and head up the coast toward Roanoke Island. The three remaining vessels, *Hopewell*, *Moonlight*, and the prize ship, "stood to Sea for to gaine the helpe of the currant [the Gulf Stream] which runneth much swifter a farre off then in sight of the coast." A postscript by White, in which he noted that from the southern tip of Florida to Virginia "all along the shore are none but eddie currants, setting to the South and Southwest," is described by Quinn as "the earliest recorded observation of the coastal counter current." (During the ensuing centuries of sail power, southbound vessels hugged the shore to take advantage of this counter current, while those bound north picked up the Gulf Stream current farther off shore.)

Just one day out on this northerly course the prize ship left the other vessels "without taking leave of our Admirall or consort, and sayled directly for England." For the two remaining vessels the weather turned exceptionally bad on August 1, "with much raine, thundering, and great spouts, which fell round about us nigh unto our ships." Governor White, even then, may have felt a premonition. Three days later they sighted the "Low sandie Ilands West of Wokokon," but "the weather continued so exceeding foule, that we could not come to an anker nye the coast: wherefore we stood off againe to Sea untill Monday the 9 of August." When the storm finally subsided, crewmen from the two vessels landed on a "narrow sandy Iland" near Wococon, where they remained three days and took in fresh water and caught a "great store of fish in the shallow water." Finally moving up the coast again, they reached "the Northeast end of the Iland of Croatoan," above modern Cape Hatteras, at nightfall on August 12, and on the following day they sounded a newly discovered inlet. On August 15, in the evening, the two ships "came to anker at Hatorask."

Governor White had returned home to Virginia three years after his departure. His journal entry that evening was full of hope and anticipation. "At our first comming to anker on this shore," he wrote, "we saw a great smoke rise in the Ile Raonoak neere the place where I left our Colony in the yeere 1587, which smoake put us in good hope that some of the Colony were there expecting my returne out of England."

CHAPTER 17

The Lost Colony

The captains of the two vessels that had reached the Outer Banks, Abraham Cooke of *Hopewell* and Edward Spicer of *Moonlight*, were justifiably wary as they approached the dangerous coast opposite Roanoke Island. In order to avoid any possibility of striking an underwater shoal they dropped anchor that first night some three miles offshore in five fathoms (thirty feet) of water.

Early the next morning—August 16, 1590—crewmen began stowing guns, powder, shot, food, equipment, and empty water casks in the two ship's boats riding alongside. *Hopewell*'s master gunner was ordered to load three of his guns and to "shoot them off with reasonable space betweene every shot, to the ende that their reportes might bee heard to the place where wee hoped to finde some of our people." It seemed an appropriate beginning for this day so long anticipated.

As soon as the two small boats shoved off for shore, Captain Cooke began taking soundings, and for the first two miles he found that the water was even deeper than where he had anchored. The smoke seen the preceding evening coming from Roanoke Island was no longer visible, but by the time the boats were halfway to shore Governor White reported seeing "another great smoke" south of the inlet, near a large Outer Banks sand hill they called Kindrikers or Kenricks "mountes." Thinking that this fire might have been started by the colonists standing watch on the coast, the governor and the two captains changed their plans and "therefore thought good to goe to that second smoke first." This proved to be a costly error, for as they trudged down the sandy banks island toward Kenricks Mount, they began to realize that it was "much further from the harbour where we landed, then we supposed it to be, so that we were very sore tired before wee came to the smoke." They were further disappointed to find "no man nor signe that any had bene there lately, nor yet any fresh water in all this way to drinke."

Tired, sore, hot, and thirsty, the men wearily retraced their steps and, on reaching the boats at the inlet, "deferred our going to Roanoak untill the next morning." Thus a day had been wasted in the fruitless trek down the sandy beach to investigate the fire near Kenricks Mount, and the decision to go there first, instead of proceeding directly to Roanoke Island, would have far-reaching consequences.

White does not give any information as to who accompanied him on the tiring beach walk, but there was among the men who remained with the boats at the inlet at least one individual who understood that beneath such barrier islands is a pocket of fresh water, the accumulation of many years of rainfall. The men were ordered to "digge in those sandie hilles for fresh water," of which White later reported, "we found very sufficient." There was not time before darkness set in, however, to fill all of the casks and load them aboard the boats.

That night, attempting to sleep on *Hopewell*, Governor White no doubt tossed and turned, frustrated over the events of the day just past, yet filled with anticipation at the prospect of what the next day might bring. In the early morning light the two ships weighed anchor and moved in closer to shore, but when Captain Cooke and White were about ready to head again for Roanoke Island, they learned that Spicer had sent his boat ashore for fresh water, so the departure was delayed for several hours. White's log states that it was "ten of the clocke aforenoone" before Cooke's boat finally put off for shore with fifteen men aboard. They were halfway in and approaching the inlet before Spicer, having hauled the water casks on board *Moonlight*, was seen to follow.

Permanent residents of the Outer Banks learn early on that changes in wind and weather can occur so quickly and so unexpectedly along the coast above Cape Hatteras that it is foolhardy to postpone important outdoor activities, even for a day, for there is no telling what the morrow will bring. On August 17, 1590, what it brought was a strong northeaster, which quickly built up huge swells offshore to crash on the beach and pound over the shoals in the inlets. One massive wave broke over Cooke's little boat as it crossed the bar, half filling the craft with water. The occupants reached shore safely only through "the will of God and carefull styrage of Captaine Cooke."

Even as Cooke's boat was being beached, and the food and guns and equipment hauled ashore to dry, Captain Spicer's boat was approaching the dangerous inlet opening. There was no perceptible channel, for "the Sea brake extremely on the barre, and the tide went very forcibly at the entrance." Halfway through the inlet, "by the rash and undiscreet styrage of Ralph Skinner his Masters mate, a very dangerous Sea brake into their boate and overset them." Some of the eleven men on board tried to hang on to the overturned craft. Others attempted to swim free. But in the shallow, shoaly water, with the waves crashing down on top of them, "the next sea set the boat on ground, where it beat so, that some of them were forced to let goe their hold, hoping to wade ashore, but the Sea still beate them downe, so that they could neither stand nor swimme, and the boat twise or thrise was turned the keele upward."

Four of the distressed mariners "were saved by Captain Cookes meanes, who so soone as he saw their oversetting, stripped himselfe, and foure other that could swimme very well, & with all haste possible rowed unto them." The rest were not so fortunate. "Captaine Spicer and Skinner hung untill they sunke, & seene no more." The remaining five disappeared also, and were presumed drowned. Of the eleven men who just moments before had entered the inlet in the small boat seven were lost. It was the forerunner of many other disasters that were to occur in succeeding centuries along that isolated stretch of coast destined to become known as the "Graveyard of the Atlantic."

What irony! More men lost their lives in those few terrifying moments at the inlet than had died among Lane's colonists in the course of the entire year they spent in Virginia. As for Edward Spicer, he had survived the harrowing return voyage on his flyboat in 1587 and months of privateering in the Spanish Caribbean, only to perish in the wreck of a boat so small it could be carried on the deck of his *Moonlight*.

Spicer's boat finally floated clear of the breakers and was hauled up on the beach. Miraculously, the sturdy little craft had suffered no appreciable damage. But seven of the twenty-six men who had set out for Roanoke Island a short while before were missing, and the survivors had mixed feelings as to the next move. White, of course, was anxious to proceed across the sound to Roanoke Island, but the seamen had other ideas. "The mischance did so much discomfort the saylors," White said, "that they were all of one mind not to goe any further to seeke the planters."

What a devastating blow for John White. After three years of frustration and disappointment, of thrice boarding ships for the voyage to Virginia, of privation and trauma, battle wounds and near-starvation, he found himself actually within sight of Roanoke Island at last, yet denied passage across that one remaining narrow body of water. But there was yet hope, for one other man among the nineteen was on his side: Captain Cooke. Together they tried to persuade the recalcitrant seamen, but persuasion was not enough. Cooke then took another approach, issuing a direct order—a "commandement" was the word White used. Some of the men wavered in their resolve, but finally, according to White, "seeing the Captaine and me so resolute, they seemed much more willing."

By then it was late evening on the Outer Banks, and when at last the two boats headed toward Roanoke Island, the sun was setting in the distance. Night fell as they crossed the sound, and by the time they approached the spot "where our planters were left, it was so exceeding darke, that we overshot the place a quarter of a mile." From the boats they "espied towards the North end of the Iland ye light of a great fire thorow the woods, to the which we presently rowed," but feeling it would be foolhardy to land in the darkness, they anchored there and prepared to spend the night huddled in the boats. In the hope that the fire had been set by the colonists as a signal, they sounded their trumpets and throughout the night sang "familiar English tunes of Songs, and called to them friendly." To some it might have seemed as much a funeral dirge for the seven who had lost their lives that day at the inlet as it was a message of hope.

Landing at daybreak the next morning, they approached the smoldering fires, finding "the grasse & sundry rotten trees burning about the place" but no sign of human beings. They then crossed the island on foot to the west side "directly over against Dasamongwepeuk," but they were equally frustrated there and returned "round about the Northpoint of the Iland," seeing only "in the sand the print of the Salvages feet."

They finally arrived at the spot where the colonists had been left, and White's log contains this description of what they found: "As we entred up the sandy banke upon a tree, in the very browe thereof were curiously carved these faire Romane letters CRO: which letters presently we knew to signifie the place, where I should find the planters seated, according to a secret token agreed upon betweene them & me at my last departure from them." White therefore assumed that his colony had abandoned the Roanoke Island base, as intended, moving some fifty miles southward to Croatoan, near Cape Hatteras.

This was further confirmed when they passed on toward the place where the colonists had been "left in sundry houses." There they found that the settlers had enclosed the area with "a high palisado of great trees, with cortynes and flankers very Fort-like." As they entered the fortified settlement, White saw that "one of the chiefe trees or postes at the right side of the entrance had the barke taken off, and 5. foote from the ground in fayre Capitall letters was graven C R O A T O A N without any crosse or signe of distress."

Once inside the palisade they found "the houses taken downe" and "many barres of Iron, two pigges of Lead, foure yron fowlers, Iron sackershotte, and such like heavie things, throwen here and there, almost overgrowen with grasse and weedes." Taking a few men with him, White then "went along by the water side, towards the poynt of the Creeke to see if we could find any of their botes or Pinnisse, but we could perceive no signe of them, nor any of the last Falkons and small Ordinance which were left with them, at my departure from them."

Returning again to the palisaded settlement, White learned that some of the sailors had "found where divers chests had bene hidden, and long sithence digged up againe and broken up, and much of the goods in them spoyled and scattered about, but nothing left, of such things as the Savages knew any use of, undefaced." In addition, in an old trench, they found five chests that had been carefully hidden by the colonists, including three belonging to Governor White. These, too, had been discovered by the Indians and broken open. This was exactly what White had been afraid might happen when he expressed his reluctance three years earlier to return to En-

gland for supplies. With obvious disappointment he reported finding "many of my things spoyled and broken,
and my bookes torne from the covers, the frames of some
of my pictures and Mappes rotten and spoyled with rayne,
and my armour almost eaten through with rust."

It was August 18, 1590. By coincidence, White had returned to his Roanoke Island settlement exactly three
years to the day after the birth there, in 1587, of his granddaughter, Virginia Dare. There would be no reunion with
the child on her third birthday, but it was typical of
White's resilience that he was able to accept the inevitable, and rationalize. "Although it much grieved me to
see such spoyle of my goods," he said, "yet on the other
side I greatly joyed that I had safely found a certaine token
of their safe being at Croatoan, which is the place where
Manteo was borne, and the Savages of the Iland our
friends."

There was no need to remain longer on Roanoke Island,
for, obviously, the next move was to get to Croatoan as
quickly as possible. Accordingly, they returned to the anchored ships "with as much speede as we could: For the
weather beganne to overcast, and very likely that a foule
and stormie night would ensue." How right he was. That
"same Evening with much danger and labour, we got our
selves aboard, by which time the winde and seas were so
greatly risen, that wee doubted our Cables and Anchors
would scarcely holde untill Morning." At that moment
someone remembered that six men had been left on shore,
on "the little Iland on the right hand of the Harbour,"
where they had been filling casks with fresh water.
"Wherefore the Captaine caused the Boate to be manned
with five lusty men, who could swimme all well," and
sent them ashore to pick up the men and their water
casks. They made it safely, rescuing the six stranded seamen, but because the waves were so high and the weather
so rough they were unable to retrieve the water casks and
left them on the island.

Hopewell and *Moonlight* rode at anchor off the Outer

Banks that night, pitching and rolling with such fury and abandon that there was real danger they would slip their anchors and be driven to certain destruction on the beach. As soon as there was sufficient daylight to observe conditions properly, "it was agreed by the Captaine and my selfe, with the Master and others, to wey anchor, and goe for the place at Croatoan, where our planters were."

There was clear logic in the decision to leave the anchorage and head south the few short leagues to Croatoan in search of the colonists. Not only would they be risking shipwreck by remaining longer at anchor off Hatorask, but as White pointed out, Croatoan was the logical destination, since the northeast wind "was good for that place." When the storm had passed and the seas had calmed, it would be a simple matter to return for the water casks.

But *Hopewell* almost didn't make it. The strong gusty winds and high ocean swells had put extra pressure on the cable, causing the anchor to sink more firmly into the sandy bottom until, in effect, it was stuck in the sand. The almost inevitable result, as the crewmen tried to haul the cable aboard the lurching vessel, was that it snapped, and *Hopewell*, out of control, drifted rapidly toward the beach. Frantically, they dropped another anchor overboard, but for the second time the cable snapped. Finally a third one, the last anchor left on the ship, took hold. By that time *Hopewell* was almost aground on the beach opposite Kenricks Mount and certainly would have been lost had she not "fallen into a chanel of deeper water," one of the innumerable ever-shifting sloughs so common off the Outer Banks. The hand of Providence had saved them, but with the storm growing ever worse Captain Cooke's main concern was to get clear of that treacherous coast as rapidly as possible. Somehow he was able to get underway and head for the open sea.

As a result of the failure to make contact with the colonists on Roanoke Island, the drowning of the seven men in

Spicer's boat crew, and the harrowing experience of the morning off Kenricks Mount, there was strong feeling among the crewmen that no further effort should be made to search for the settlers at Croatoan. Some pressed for an immediate return to England while it was still early enough in the season and the ships were sufficiently seaworthy to make the crossing. But White and Captain Cooke proposed that they sail south to the Caribbean, where they could get fresh water and food and perhaps even take another prize from which back-up cables and anchors could be removed.

It was one thing for the two leaders aboard *Hopewell*, Captain Cooke and Governor White, to convince their crewmen that such a course would enable them "to make 2. rich voyages of one," continuing to carry on their profitable privateering while wintering in the West Indies, then sailing back up the coast to Croatoan in the early spring. But the reaction aboard *Moonlight* was quite different. With Captain Spicer dead, the vessel was under command of acting captain John Bedford, and he and his crew were convinced that their "weake and leake Shippe was not able to continue it." That night the two vessels parted, *Moonlight* setting a course for England and home, and *Hopewell*, for Trinidad, the island finally selected as their winter base.

Hopewell encountered even more adversity long before nearing its destination. "The winde changed, and it was sette on foule weather every way," with conditions so bad that the vessel was "able to beare no sayle, but our forecourse halfe mast high." *Hopewell* was forced to ride for days before the storm-driven winds, moving all the while not toward the Caribbean but across the open sea.

By the time the storm subsided, it was necessary once again for Cooke and White to make a change in plans. Their reserve supply of food and water was seriously depleted, and since they were already far out in the Atlantic they decided to head for the Azores. Not only would they be able to take on water, but possibly, with luck, they could "meete with some English men of warre about those Ilands, at whose hands wee might obtaine some supply of our wants."

Hopewell reached the Azores September 17, almost a month after the departure from the Outer Banks. The first vessel sighted was a large Spanish ship, which turned out to be a prize taken by *Hopewell*'s late vice-admiral, *Little John*. Two days later, "neere a small village on the North side of Flores," they found five English men-of-war riding at anchor. One of the five was "*Moonelight* our consort, who upon the first sight of our comming into Flores, set sayle and went for England, not taking any leave of us." Obviously, Captain Bedford and his crew were taking no chances of being pressed into service by Captain Cooke and White for a return that year to Virginia.

The sight of the large prize vessel taken by *Little John*, and of *Moonlight* sneaking away toward England before contact could be made, apparently proved too much for the men aboard *Hopewell*. Once more the plan was changed. Instead of returning to the West Indies that fall, and on to Virginia and Croatoan the next spring, they decided to head back to England, where they could claim their share of the prize money.

Thus ended Governor John White's drawn-out three-year effort to return to his planters, his assistants, and his family in Virginia. White, always the optimist, had given up. He must have assumed that his settlers were safe, and happy too, in their new life with Manteo and his friendly tribesmen at Croatoan.

White may have been right. But, for the record, those 116 English men, women, and children abandoned on the vast North American continent in 1587 simply disappeared—to be known forever as Sir Walter Raleigh's "lost colony."

CHAPTER 18

Searching for the Colonists

Beginning with John White's frustrated efforts to make contact with his settlers at Croatoan in 1590, the search for the Roanoke Island planters has gone on for nearly four hundred years.

Innumerable clues, some substantive and others nothing more than intriguing bits and pieces of information, have come to light. One after another the leads have been tracked down, often producing still more clues and avenues of investigation—or exasperating dead ends. During Raleigh's lifetime men searched for the colonists themselves, always hoping to find at least some of them alive. Since then the hope has been to find sure signs of their fate. Explorers, historians, archaeologists, mystery buffs, amateur detectives, novelists, playwrights, charlatans, and quacks have shared in the search.

This effort has produced a wide assortment of books, pamphlets, and articles, each purporting to offer conclusive proof to support one or another theory. Did the colonists, as White surmised, leave Roanoke Island to take up permanent residence with the Croatoan Indians near Cape Hatteras? If so, are their descendants still living on the North Carolina Outer Banks? Or did they move farther into the interior, joining Menatonon's Chawanoacs? Or to the north, to live with the Chesepeians? Or to the southwest, where the Indians in North Carolina's Robeson County have claimed descent from Sir Walter Raleigh's colonists?

Some have contended that they were wiped out by disease—or by famine. Others advance the theory that they attempted to return to England in one of the small vessels left them by White, only to disappear in the vastness of the Atlantic. Still others are convinced that they were attacked and killed by Wanchese and the Roanoacs, or by the Indians of Powhatan's Jamestown-area confederacy, or by the Spaniards.

Today's reader has an opportunity to sort out the clues and come up with at least a partial answer. Historians have undertaken more research on the subject in the past four decades than in the preceding three and a half centuries. These researchers have uncovered previously unknown or misplaced records, principally in the archives of England and Spain, that shed new light on the Raleigh colonies, and on the Indians and Spaniards of that period. The scholars who have studied the evidence most carefully have finally reached agreement, in part at least, on what probably happened or did not happen to the lost colonists. The conclusions of those authorities are forthcoming, but the evidence comes first—evidence with which the reader can make his own effort to solve the mystery of Sir Walter Raleigh's lost colony.

The search for information is picked up, logically, following White's return to England in late 1590 after finding his Roanoke Island settlement abandoned. White—father, grandfather, and governor of the colony—probably planned to return again to search for the planters, but he appears to have been thwarted by an inability to secure the necessary backing. In a letter to Richard Hakluyt in early 1593 he appeared to give up, stating that relief of the colony was left "to the merciful help of the Almighty." He then added this poignant comment: "I would to God my wealth were answerable to my will."

Sir Walter Raleigh, on the other hand, possessed the

wealth, but seemed to lack the will. By 1590, when his patent of discovery expired, he appears to have lost interest in Virginia. In retrospect, the Roanoke Island venture seems to have been not much more than another speculative business deal for the man to whom Queen Elizabeth had granted exclusive rights to much of the New World.

In 1591, the year after White's return, Raleigh backed another privateering expedition in American waters by John Watts, again involving the ships *Hopewell*, *Little John*, and possibly even *John Evangelist*. The Watts venture, however, failed to make so much as a cursory search for the lost colonists; in fact there is no indication that Raleigh even asked him to. The expedition did produce a profit for the backers, but Raleigh still complained that the return was too small for the investment. "Wee might have gotten more to have sent them a fishing," he said.

In 1595, Sir Walter himself finally sailed to America, but the course he set was not to Virginia and Roanoke Island. Instead he explored the South American coast, much of which was then known as Guiana, and specifically the Orinoco River in modern Venezuela. His interest in American colonization thus renewed, Raleigh proceeded to write a book, *The Discoverie of Guiana*, which was published the following year. In 1598 he tried again to assemble a fleet for a voyage to Guiana, this one a large flotilla of some thirteen vessels, but was unsuccessful.

Finally, in 1602, fifteen years after the Roanoke Island colony was abandoned, Raleigh decided to renew his search for the planters. According to John Brereton, he sent over one Samuel Mace, an experienced mariner, "who had been at Virginia twice before." Though the avowed purpose of this venture was to search for the lost colony, skeptics have charged that, since Raleigh's patent had expired, this effort was an attempt to keep it in force by claiming that his Roanoke Island planters still occupied Virginia soil. Finding them alive was a key to validating his old patent.

In an apparent attempt to prevent Mace and the crew of

his small bark from spending their time in privateering activities, Raleigh hired them for monthly wages. Mace attempted a direct crossing of the Atlantic instead of taking the circuitous but more common Caribbean route, and missed his mark badly. He made his landfall "fortie leagues to the southwestward of Hatarask, in thirty foure degrees or thereabout," which would have put him in the immediate vicinity of Cape Fear. He and his men dawdled there for a month, trading with the natives for roots and herbs, including sassafras, which then commanded a high price on the London market. Finally, they headed north along the coast, but instead of searching for the lost colonists they returned to England, claiming that "the extremitie of weather and losse of some principall ground-tackle, forced and feared them from searching the port of Hatarask, the isle of Croatan, or any parte of the Mayne of Dasamonguepeuk." As had John White many years earlier, they returned with no information at all as to the fate of the lost colony.

Raleigh was in no position to follow up on the Mace venture, even if he had wanted to, for he was soon to be charged with treason, convicted, and imprisoned in the Tower of London. Others, however, took up where he had left off in the exploration and exploitation of North America. Even as Mace was loading his bark with Cape Fear sassafras in 1602, Bartholomew Gosnold was attempting to establish a fur-trading base in the vicinity of Cuttyhunk Island, off the Massachusetts coast. Meanwhile, Bartholomew Gilbert sailed to Virginia with the intent of exploring the Chesapeake, only to be killed by Indians, and Martin Pring, with backing from Hakluyt, visited the Cape Cod area. Even more active was Samuel de Champlain, who made several crossings of the Atlantic between 1604 and 1606, concentrating on exploration of the New England coast, while others attempted to establish the Sagadahoc colony in Canada.

By then the saga of Raleigh's Virginia colonization effort

had ended. But despite his apparent lack of concern or compassion for the settlers abandoned on Roanoke Island, Raleigh is credited almost universally with planting the seed that led to the successful settlement of much of North America by the English. The men who established that first permanent settlement at Jamestown in 1607 were fully aware that a colony of English men, women, and children had been left on Roanoke Island twenty years earlier, and they made repeated efforts to seek them out.

One of the leaders of the Jamestown colony, George Percy, describing an expedition into the Virginia interior in May 1607, made the following comment about a discovery at a place thought to have been located on the James River some twenty miles below the falls: "*At Port Cotage in our Voyage up the River, we saw a Savage Boy about the age of ten yeeres, which had a head of haire of a perfect yellow and a reasonable white skinne, which is a Miracle amongst all Savages.*" For more than a century history sleuths have cited this as the first bit of evidence that descendants of the lost colonists were still living in Virginia when the Jamestown colony arrived.

Captain John Smith, later the Jamestown president, made several references to the lost colonists in his book *A True Relation of such occurrences and accidents of noate as hath hapned in Virginia since the first planting of that Collony.* Of a meeting with the king of the Pamunkey Indians, he had this to say: "*What he knew of the dominions he spared not to acquaint me with, as of certaine men cloathed at a place called Ocanahonan, cloathed like me.*"

Later, in his travels into the interior, at a place called Weramocomoco, the local Indian chief, or "Emperour," as Smith described him, gave still more information. "*Many Kingdomes hee described mee. . . . The people cloathed at Ocamahowan, he also confirmed; and the Southerly Countries also, as the rest that reported us to be within a day and a halfe of Mangoge, two dayes of Chawwonock,*

6. *from Roonock, to the south part of the backe sea: He described a countrie called Anone, where they have abundance of Brasse, and houses walled as ours."*

Smith's interest was sufficiently whetted for him to send a delegation in search of the people who dressed like the English and lived in English-style houses, with the following results: *"We had agreed with the king of Paspahegh, to conduct two of our men to a place called Panawicke beyond Roonok, where he reported many men to be apparelled. Wee landed him at Warraskoyack, where playing the villaine, and deluding us for rewards, returned within three or foure dayes after, without going further."*

This attempt to make contact with the lost colonists was mentioned again, in a 1610 report prepared by the governors and councilors of the Jamestown colony. *"If with these we compare the advantages which we have gotten, in the shortness and security of the passage, in the intelligence of some of our Nation planted by Sir Walter Raleigh, yet a live, within fifty mile of our fort, who can open the womb and bowels of this country; as is testified by two of our colony sent out to seek them, who, (though denied by the savages speech with them) found crosses and Letters the Characters and assured Testimonies of Christians newly cut in the barks of trees."*

Through the years historians must have spent thousands of hours trying to identify the places mentioned by Smith in the above references. One of the problems is that, lacking a dictionary, those who wrote the accounts of early English colonization seemed to have had little concern for consistency in spelling. Thus Smith refers once to "Ocanahonan" and later the same name is spelled "Ocamahowan," "Ocanahawan," and "Ochanahoen." John Smith's talents with pen and paper, however, were not limited to writing, for he was an accomplished cartographer as well, and in 1608 he sent back to England a chart he had prepared showing the areas of Virginia he had visited and heard about.

Three notations on the chart are considered key evidence in the lost colony mystery. At a place generally thought to have been on the Neuse or Tar rivers in modern North Carolina, Smith made this notation: *"Here remayneth 4 men clothed that came from Roonock to Ocanahawan."* More to the north and west is the following: *"Here the King of Paspahege reported our men to be and wants to go."* The final notation appears in the vicinity of the James River. *"Here Paspahege and 2 of our own men landed to go to Pananiock."*

These seemingly oblique references to the lost colonists by George Percy and John Smith were substantiated and elaborated upon by other participants in the early Jamestown venture. One of the most telling pieces of information was contained in a series of instructions sent from England in May, 1609, by the council of the Virginia Company to the governor at Jamestown. The council proposed establishing a "principall and chiefe seate," or headquarters, for the permanent Virginia colony near *"a towne called Ohonahorn seated where the River of Choanocki devideth it self into three braunches and falleth into the sea of Rawnocke."*

Extolling the virtues of this site, generally conceded to have been on the west side of the Chowan River in what is now Bertie County, North Carolina, the council concluded as follows: *"Besides you are neere to Riche Copper mines of Ritanoc and may passe them by one braunche of this River, and by another Peccarecamicke where you shall finde foure of the englishe alive, left by Sr. Walter Rawely which escaped from the slaughter of Powhaton of Roanocke, uppon the first arrival of our Colonie, and live under the proteccōn of a wiroane called Gepanocon enemy to Powhaton, by whose consent you shall never recover them."*

Raleigh's colonists slaughtered by Powhatan? Others mentioned this as well, beginning with a notation in the margin of a volume entitled *Hakluytus Posthumus, or Purchas His Pilgrimes.* "*Powatan confessed that he had been at the murder of that colony, and showed a musket barrel and a brass mortar, and certain pieces of iron which had been theirs.*"

Still more information comes from William Strachey, who sailed for Jamestown in 1609 and served for several years as secretary of the colony. Back again in England in 1612 he prepared an extensive and detailed report entitled *The Historie of Travell Into Virginia Britania,* with the following references to Raleigh's lost colonists: "*At Peccarecanick, and Ochanahoen, by the Relation of Machumps, the People have howses built with stone walls, and one story above another, so taught them by those English who escaped the slaughter at Roanoak. . . . At Ritanoe, the Weroance Eyanoco preserved 7. of the English alive, fower men, twoo Boyes, and one young Maid, (who escaped and fled up the River of Chanoke) to beat his Copper, of which he hath certayn Mynes at the said Ritanoe.*"

The areas described in these references—Peccarecanick, Ochanahoen, and Ritanoe—were located in what Strachey referred to as the "high-land" of Virginia. Concerning the "low-land," which extended southward along the Atlantic Ocean from Chesapeake Bay to Florida, he had this to say: "*In this Countrey it was that Sir Walter Raleigh planted his twoo Colonies, in the Island aforesaid called Roanoak.*" He then dealt at length with Powhatan, including the following reference: "*He doth often send unto us to temporize with us, awayting perhapps but a fitt opportunity (inflamed by his bloudy and furious priests) to offer us a tast of the same Cuppe which he made our poore Countrymen drinck off at Roanoak.*"

Strachey went on to give more of the specifics of Powhatan's encounter with the Roanoke Island settlers.

"*His Majestie hath bene acquainted, that the men women, and Children of the first plantation at Roanoak were by practize and Comaundement of Powhatan (he himself perswaded thereunto by his Priests) miserably slaughtered without any offence given him . . . by the first planted (who 20. and od yeares had peaceably lyved and intermixed with those Savadges, and were out of his Territory).*"

John Smith made yet another reference to the search for the lost colony in his *Description of Virginia*, published in 1612. "*Southward they went to some parts of Chawonock and the Mangoags, to search them there left by Sir Walter Raleigh; for those parts to the Towne of Chisapeack, hath formerly been discovered by Mr. Heriots and Sir Raph Layne.*"

The final clues in the literature of the Jamestown settlement appeared in a report prepared by several leaders of the colony and published in 1612 under the title *The Proceedings of the English Colony in Virginia*. In referring to one of Captain Smith's journeys mention is made of his dealings with an Indian chief. "*The Captaine thanked him for his good counsell, yet the better to try his love, desired guides to Chowanoke, for he would sent a present to that king to bind him his friend. To performe this journey was sent Michael Sicklemore, a very honest, valiant, and painefull soldier: with him, two guids, and directions howe to search for the lost company of Sir Walter Rawley, and silke grasse.*"

The results of Michael Sicklemore's journey are given later in the report, together with reference to yet another search party. "*Mr. Sicklemore well returned from Chawonock, but found little hope and lesse certainetie of them [that] were left by Sir Walter Rawley. So that Nathaniell Powell and Anas Todkill were also, by the Quiyoughquohanocks, conducted to the Mangoages to search them there. But nothing could we learne but they were all dead.*"

This mention of specific individuals—Michael Sickle-more, Nathaniell Powell, and Anas Todkill—who journeyed into the southern part of Virginia in an effort to find the lost colony is the last reference to Raleigh's planters by those who settled Jamestown.

The chain of evidence in the mystery does not pick up again for more than forty years, at which time Virginia Dare would have been in her sixties if still alive.

CHAPTER 19

Clues and Theories

It is not at all difficult to understand why Captain John Smith and his settlers, in the first years following their arrival at Jamestown in 1607, made repeated efforts to contact the Roanoke Island colonists. Concern for the plight of fellow Englishmen may have played a part, and plain, ordinary curiosity; but the real motivation was their own self-preservation. They were attempting to establish a permanent English colony in a new and alien land, surrounded by hostile natives under the domination of a leader, Powhatan, who had vowed to wipe out their settlement.

Obviously, they had carefully studied Hariot's detailed description of the lands and people of Virginia, as well as the Barlowe, Lane, and White narratives published by Hakluyt. But this was information based on observations made nearly a quarter of a century earlier. The survivors of Roanoke Island, if some could be found alive, would be in a position to provide them with up-to-date information and guidance based on many years of continuous residence in Virginia.

By 1612, just five years after reaching Jamestown, they had given up the search, convinced that none of the lost colonists remained alive. From that time on, the Virginia planters, and those who settled adjacent areas throughout the remaining years of the seventeenth century, had more pressing matters on their minds, and the effort to find survivors of Roanoke Island was ended. Consequently, for nearly two and a half centuries thereafter, the historical annals contain only incidental references to the lost colony, most by people who visited or wanted to visit Lane's fort.

Probably the earliest post-Jamestown reference to the Roanoke Island settlement was contained in a letter written in 1654 by a prominent Virginia planter named Francis Yeardley.

> *In September last, a young man, a trader for beavers, being bound out to the adjacent parts to trade, by accident his sloop left him; and he, supposing she had been gone to Rhoanoke, hired a small boat. . . . They entered in at Caratoke, ten leagues to the southward of Cape Henry, and so went to Rhoanoke island; where, or near thereabouts, they found the great commander of those parts with his Indians a hunting, who received them civilly, and shewed them the ruins of Sir Walter Ralegh's fort, from whence I received a sure token of their being there.*

In 1660, a Reverend Morgan Jones was reported to have preached in the Neuse River area to Indians who were light colored and supposedly spoke Welsh. Ten years later, in his travels through lower Virginia, the explorer John Lederer visited an area near a lake called Ushery, where "*a powerful Nation of Bearded men were seated, which I suppose to be the Spaniards, because the Indians never have any.*"

It was not until 1709 that a direct reference to the lost colonists, and a hint of their possible fate, appeared in print. This was in *A New Voyage to Carolina* by John Lawson, surveyor-general of the Carolina colony. He begins with a reference to Lane's fort.

> *The first Discovery and Settlement of this Country was by the Procurement of Sir Walter Raleigh, in Conjunction with some publick-spirited Gentlemen of that Age, under the Protection of Queen Elizabeth; for which Reason it was then named Virginia, being begun on that part called Roanoak-Island, where the Ruins of a Fort are to be seen at this day, as well as some old English Coins which have been lately found; and a Bras-Gun, a Powder-Horn, and one small Quarter deck-Gun, made of Iron Staves, and hoop'd with the same Metal; which Method of making Guns might very probably be made use of in those Days, for the Convenience of Infant-Colonies.*

Lawson then became the first of many historians to offer his own ideas concerning the possible fate of the lost colony.

> *A farther Confirmation of this we have from the Hatteras Indians, who either then lived on Ronoak-Island, or much frequented it. These tell us, that several of their Ancestors were white People, and could talk in a Book, as we do; the Truth of which is confirm'd by gray Eyes being found frequently amongst these Indians, and no others. They value themselves extremely for their Affinity to the English, and are ready to do them all friendly Offices. It is probable, that this Settlement miscarry'd for want of timely Supplies from England; or thro' the Treachery of the Natives, for we may reasonably suppose that the English were forced to cohabit with them, for Relief and Conversation; and that in process of Time, they conform'd themselves to the Manners of their Indian Relations. And thus we see, how apt Humane Nature is to degenerate.*

One of the things that makes Lawson's account such interesting reading is that he did not limit himself to the results of his own personal observations or to information received second-hand from the Indians. He even delved into Indian folklore. *"I cannot forbear inserting here, a pleasant Story that passes for an uncontested Truth amongst the Inhabitants of this Place; which is, that the Ship which brought the first Colonies, does often appear amongst them, under Sail, in a gallant Posture, which they call Sir Walter Raleigh's Ship; And the truth of this has been affirm'd to me, by Men of the best Credit in the Country."*

Though Roanoke Island was settled by the time Lawson appeared on the scene, and an act of the North Carolina Colonial Assembly in 1723 provided for establishing a town on the island near what was referred to as "Roanoke old plantation," the only other direct reference to the settlement prior to the Revolution was the appearance of the word *fort* near the northeastern tip of Roanoke Island on the 1770 Collet map of North Carolina.

In 1819 a president of the United States visited the Cittie of Ralegh site. In early April, President James Monroe left Washington "on a tour southward," primarily to inspect coastal defenses and waterways. The presidential party, by this time including a number of prominent North Carolinians, toured the sounds in the steamboat *Albemarle*. On April 6 they inspected the site of old Roanoke Inlet at Nags Head and anchored that night off the northern end of Roanoke Island. The following morning, according to the *Edenton Gazette*, President Monroe and his entourage landed on Roanoke Island *"to view the remains of the Fort, the traces of which are still distinctly visible, which is said to have been erected by the first colony of Sir Walter Raleigh."*

Though historian Francis X. Martin mentioned in his 1829 *History of North Carolina* that the stump of a live oak said to have been the tree on which White found carved the letters CRO *"was shown as late as the year 1778 by the people of Roanoke Island,"* he made no effort to speculate on the fate of the lost colonists. In 1857, however, Francis L. Hawks devoted the first volume of his two-volume *History of North Carolina* exclusively to Raleigh's colonies. After reprinting the accounts from Hakluyt and de Bry, Hawks concluded the book with a statement that the lack of incentive for individual ownership of property and too little attention paid "to individual character in the selection of the colonists" contributed to the failure of White's settlement. He then gave his own opinion as to what happened to the colonists: *"But we are inclined to think that these causes would not have prevented the successful establishment of White's colony, had it not been subjected to the horrors of famine. Time and experience would probably have corrected the evils we have named; but for starvation there was no remedy."*

Three years after the publication of Hawks's history, Edward C. Bruce recounted, in an article in the May, 1860, issue of *Harper's New Monthly Magazine*, his visit to the site of Lane's fort. *"The trench is clearly traceable in a square forty yards each way,"* he said, with the ditch *"generally two feet deep,"* though the whole fortification was overgrown with trees and vines. Bruce had studied his history lessons, and he was obviously impressed with what had taken place on Roanoke Island. *"The thought will often arise that, though Smith was the man, Raleigh ought to have been,"* he said. He then mentioned something that still troubles those who would memorialize the first English colony in America: *"How many of us can, at a minute's notice, point out Roanoke Island on the map? Plymouth, Jamestown, and St. Augustine spring at once to the finger's end. But that lonely isle in Albemarle Sound is so unfamiliar that the mapmakers often forget to label it."*

Soon after the appearance of the Bruce article, Americans were embroiled in civil war, and Roanoke Island became a Confederate stronghold, the key to resisting Federal efforts to gain control of the North Carolina sounds. A large Federal fleet attacked the island base February 7, 1862. That night an estimated 7,500 Federal troops landed under cover of darkness, and by afternoon of the next day 2,765 Confederate officers and men had been captured, and Roanoke Island was once again a part of the Union. Contrabands—former slaves from the plantations in the interior—flocked to the island, and for the next three years large numbers of Federal troops and ex-slaves were quartered on Roanoke.

With little else to occupy them on this isolated island some of the troops stationed there turned their attention to the abandoned Elizabethan colony. *"A favorite amusement of my own, whenever I could obtain a pass,"* wrote one of the soldiers, *"was to explore the island, searching for traces of, and speculating upon the fate of, that lost colony."* It was later reported that several holes were dug in the earthworks as members of the garrison searched for treasure, but, *"on complaint of Mr. Walter Dough, who then owned the fort, the vandalism was promptly checked and the fort placed under military guard."* By then a few items had been removed—a hatchet, some Indian pottery, a few small iron fragments, and possibly a vial of quicksilver—but most of the embankment apparently was left untouched.

One soldier seemed unconcerned about the fate of the colonists, but posed another question. *"How they ever found it or why those chose it as an abiding place,"* he said, *"I cannot imagine. It is easier to account for the fact that the colony was abandoned."* More than 250 years had passed since John Smith and his Jamestown settlers gave up the search for the lost colonists, and throughout that period few people had shown any interest in finding out what had happened to them. Then, with the approach of the three hundredth anniversary of the Roanoke Island settlements, a man named Hamilton McMillan came up with his own theory, and set out doggedly to prove it.

McMillan, a white man, educated and literate, was then living in the Robeson County area of southeastern North Carolina near a settlement of "persons of mixed color" sometimes known as "redbones" and long classed as mulattoes, though recognized locally as Indians. As mulattoes, they were denied access to white schools, and for the most part they flatly refused to attend the Negro schools. Thus largely uneducated, though industrious, they lived in clannish poverty, still clinging to their Indian traditions. One of these was that they were descended from an admixture of native American Indians with the earliest English settlers in a place one of them referred to as "Roanoke in Virginia."

"*The language spoken,*" McMillan later reported, "*is almost pure Anglo-Saxon,*" and he gave the following examples: "*Mon (Saxon) is used for man, father is pronounced fayther. . . . Mension is used for measurement, aks for ask, hit for it, hosen for hose, lovend for loving, housen for houses. . . . Many of the words in common use among them have long been obsolete in English-speaking countries.*"

Intrigued with the possibility that these people might truly be descendants of Raleigh's lost colony, McMillan studied the accounts from Hakluyt and found among his neighbors "*many family names identical with those of the lost colony of 1587.*" Further, the tribe of some twenty-five hundred was described by McMillan as "*a proud race, boasting alike of their English and Indian blood, hospitable to strangers, and ever ready to do friendly offices for white people.*"

McMillan was by then convinced that he had solved the mystery of the lost colony. Concerned also with the plight of the tribe, he proceeded to take their case to state officials, and finally to the North Carolina General Assembly. The result was an 1885 act "*to provide for separate schools for Croatan Indians in Robeson County,"* which read in part:

> *Whereas the Indians now living in Robeson County claim to be descendants of a friendly tribe who once resided in eastern North Carolina on the Roanoke River, known as the Croatan Indians; therefore,*
>
> *The General Assembly of North Carolina do enact:*
>
> *SECTION 1. That the said Indians and their descendants shall hereafter be designated and known as the Croatan Indians.*
>
> *SEC. 2. That said Indians and their descendants shall have separate schools for their children, school committees of their own race and color, and shall be allowed to select teachers of their own choice.*

McMillan had built a strong case, most of which he included in a booklet published in 1888. Three years later, North Carolina historian Stephen B. Weeks presented a paper, "The Lost Colony of Roanoke: Its Fate and Survival," to the American Historical Association, in which he offered further substantiation. Especially interesting was his finding that of the ninety-five different surnames found among the colonists left on Roanoke Island by John White *"forty-one, or more than forty-three per cent ... are reproduced by a tribe living hundreds of miles from Roanoke Island, and after a lapse of three hundred years."*

Another North Carolina historian, R. D. W. Connor, later to become the first to hold the position of archivist of the United States, in a 1907 treatise on the Roanoke Island settlement published by the North Carolina Historical Commission, repeated the Weeks contention that *"no other theory of their origin has been advanced, and it is confidently believed that the one here proposed is logically and historically the best."* Still the designation as

"Croatans" and the right to establish their own schools did not solve the problems facing the Robeson County Indians, and they petitioned the United States Office of Indian Affairs for official recognition of their tribal status, which resulted in an exhaustive investigation by special agent O. M. McPherson. In 1915 the findings were published in a 252-page government report, *Indians of North Carolina*. McPherson's conclusion: *"I have no hesitancy in expressing the belief that the Indians originally settled in Robeson and adjoining counties in North Carolina were an amalgamation of the Hatteras Indians with Gov. White's lost colony."*

At long last the mystery had been solved. Or had it?

For the first time, in 1887 and again in 1896, controlled excavations were undertaken at the fort site on Roanoke Island, by an archaeologist named Talcott Williams. He was able to confirm the existence of Lane's fort, but he made no effort to speculate on the lost colony mystery. Already, however, one North Carolina historian, Samuel A'Court Ashe, discounting the Robeson County evidence, seemed convinced that the colonists had moved west to the banks of the Chowan River and *"seated themselves on what are now the pleasant bluffs of Bertie County,"* far removed from McMillan's Croatans. Yet another theory was advanced in 1924 in a privately printed 547-page book, *The Conquest of Virginia—The First Attempt*, in which author Conway Whittle Sams concluded that the colonists had been attacked at the fort on Roanoke Island by the followers of both Wanchese and Powhatan. The survivors of that attack had scattered in different directions, some going to Croatan, others up the Chowan, still others up the Pamlico, and the remainder settling on the Neuse.

Another revival of interest in the lost colony accompanied the approach of the 350th anniversary of the Roanoke Island settlement. In the mid-1930s, WPA money was used to construct a chapel and other log buildings—an artist's rendering of what the Cittie of Ralegh might have looked like—in the vicinity of Lane's old fort, and in 1937, in a specially constructed waterside theater, Pulitzer-prize-winning author Paul Green's "symphonic drama" *The Lost Colony* made its premiere. (This work, the fore-runner of the modern "outdoor drama," is still being presented there each summer and is still referred to locally as "the pageant.") The Post Office Department issued a commemorative stamp, and President Roosevelt made a special visit to view *The Lost Colony*.

Playwright Green depicted the colonists abandoning the Roanoke Island base for Croatoan and left his audience to speculate on what happened thereafter. But even as the actors were packing their costumes and greasepaint after that first season, new clues and new theories were surfacing. In an article in London's *Cornhill Magazine*, Robert E. Betts concluded that the colonists were attacked by the Spaniards. *"It is possible, judging by the relations between Spain and England at that time, that the colonists were removed to Spain, tried, jailed, or put to death. Again, it may be that the Spaniards incited the Indians to slay the English."*

Betts was only offering an opinion, but down in Georgia, at Brenau College, news leaked out of discoveries that could shed an entirely new light on the lost colony. Dr. Haywood Pearce, Jr., vice president of the college, revealed that a man had brought him for identification a twenty-one pound stone found on the bank of the Chowan River near Edenton which bore an inscription apparently signed with Eleanor White Dare's initials. Subsequently, in western Georgia, a second stone had been found, and then others. In all a total of forty-nine stones had turned up, and these formed what the press referred to as "Eleanor Dare's Diary."

As more and more of the stones had surfaced, Pearce related, he had expressed continued concern as to their authenticity, but had subjected them to *"every scientific test I could command."* He reported that stonecutters said the inscriptions could not be duplicated with modern techniques. Geologists certified the age of the work. Specialists in Elizabethan English verified the authenticity of the words and script. Finally, a panel of distinguished historians visited Brenau to examine the stones and the evidence. The panel, which was led by highly respected historian Dr. Samuel Eliot Morison, announced that *"the preponderance of evidence points to the authenticity of the stones."*

As noted by Dr. Pearce, the Eleanor Dare stones did not necessarily conflict with the Robeson County theory. There was still the possibility that some of the surviving colonists settled there, as claimed by McMillan and Weeks, while others went on to the backcountry of Georgia. Not everyone, however, was convinced, especially Melvin Robinson and C. K. Howe. In 1946, in a privately published booklet, Robinson contended that the Roanoke Island of the 1580s was actually the Cedar Island of the 1940s located in the lower reaches of Pamlico Sound, and he implied that the descendants of the lost colonists were still living in that area. The next year, Howe, in another privately published booklet, revealed the discovery of *"the purported diary of Eleanor Dare, herself."* The diary and other supporting documentation indicated that the colonists had settled near the Occoneechee Mountains *"on the Eno River just south of present Hillsboro, N.C."*

Even these revelations did not end the speculation. In 1954 the University of North Carolina Press published the highly acclaimed *North Carolina: The History of a Southern State*, written by two of the state's most respected historians, Hugh Talmage Lefler and Albert Ray Newsome. They suggested yet another possible answer to the mystery. *"One of the most plausible theories— though never advanced by writers—is that the group, fi-*

nally despairing of relief, sailed for England in a boat which had been left with them by White in 1587, and were lost in the Atlantic."

This, then, is the evidence, part based on what might be considered reliable clues, the rest on pure speculation. Still other claims—including those that various remnant Indian groups, such as the Malungeons in Tennessee, were direct descendants of the colonists—have been ruled out, though speculation continues as to the origin of those known now as Haliwars, living in Halifax and Warren counties in northeastern North Carolina. From this often conflicting information those who have carried on the search most diligently are now able to draw some definite conclusions.

CHAPTER 20

What Happened to the Lost Colony?

With such a mass of lost colony clues at hand it is now necessary to weed out the less plausible ones in order to concentrate on those that seem most logical and pertinent.

Several of the claims can be laid to rest permanently, beginning with the "purported diary of Eleanor Dare, herself," which was brought to light in C. K. Howe's 1947 publication, *Solving the Riddle of the Lost Colony*. In subsequent correspondence with this writer, Howe admitted that he had been duped and was convinced that the so-called diary and other "documentation" placing the surviving colonists on the Eno River near Hillsborough consisted of nothing more than fabrications.

Similarly, the claim of Melvin Robinson that the Roanoke Island of the 1580s is actually the Cedar Island of today, with the implication that descendants of the colonists are still living there, can be discarded. The site of Lane's fort on Roanoke Island has been identified and examined by numerous individuals over a span of centuries, and extensive archaeological work under the direction of the National Park Service has confirmed the location, size, and shape of the earthwork fortifications. Further, nothing in the historical record substantiates the Cedar Island theory, and it emerges as a classic example of an individual using a biased interpretation of selected data to prove a preconceived conclusion, systematically discarding in the process all contrary evidence.

Another theory cited frequently has been put to rest as well. This is the contention that the colonists were killed by the Spaniards—either wiped out in a Roanoke Island attack or captured and returned to Spain for trial. Fortunately, nearly half a century ago, British historians began looking into the Spanish Archives in Seville for information bearing on early English colonization efforts in America, especially the Roanoke Island ventures. The official records they found show conclusively that the Spaniards were concerned about this intrusion into their established zone of influence across the Atlantic. In 1588 they searched for the settlement on Chesapeake Bay and made a landing on the Outer Banks where, near one of the larger inlets, they found water casks and "signs of a slipway for small vessels." But as late as 1600 the Spaniards were still looking for the English colony, which they believed to be on Chesapeake Bay, rather than Roanoke Island.

It is probable that no single activity has generated more interest in the lost colony than the revelation by Dr. Haywood Pearce, Jr., of the discovery of the Eleanor Dare stones in the late 1930s and early 1940s. These discoveries received nationwide publicity, though even Brenau College's Dr. Pearce made no direct claims as to their authenticity. As more and more stones turned up, the general reaction of the public was one of growing skepticism. Then, when Samuel Eliot Morison and his panel of distinguished historians journeyed to Georgia from various parts of the country to inspect the stones and the evidence offered by Pearce, that attitude changed, for the historians declared that the "preponderance of evidence points to the authenticity of the stones." They quite easily could have hedged or couched their comments in carefully coined scholarly terms. But theirs was a positive statement; they implied their belief in the validity of the stones, even if they did not exactly say that the discovery had solved the mystery of the lost colony.

In 1940, when Dr. Pearce submitted an article for publication to the *Saturday Evening Post*, the editors assigned a journalist-reporter, Boyden Sparkes, to investigate the story. Sparkes dug into crannies and crevices that the historians had not bothered to examine, and in the process he dissected the stone theory with the skill of a highly qualified surgeon.

Checking first with the authorities Pearce used in conducting what he had described as "every scientific test I could command," Sparkes found some interesting evidence that had been overlooked by or not offered to the panel of historians. The geologist, for example, had expressed great concern over the authenticity of the stones, stating categorically that at least one of the inscriptions had been carved quite recently. The authority on Elizabethan English admitted that some of the words found on the stones probably had not been introduced into the English language until centuries later. Even the stonecutters acknowledged that such work could have been faked quite easily.

Meanwhile, back on Roanoke Island, people remembered that a man who met the description of the one who found the first stone had tried several years earlier to interest local officials in buying similar stones with recently engraved antique-looking inscriptions and planting them around the areas as a publicity gimmick for *The Lost Colony*. Sparkes presented page after page of the evidence made available to the historians at Brenau College, and then systematically tore it all apart. The hoax of the Eleanor Dare stones was properly put away, once and for all.

Not so easily disposed of is the solution offered by North Carolina historian Francis L. Hawks, who seemed convinced that the colonists, beset by famine, had starved to death on the isolated Outer Banks island to which they removed. Hawks, of course, could no more offer proof than can modern-day historians prove him wrong. Like so many nonresident writers, however, he seems to have harbored the mistaken impression that all of the islands off the North Carolina coast are low, bare, windswept shoals, ever breached by storm tides. In truth, the Raleigh colonists described many of them as lush and fertile—as they still appear today—verdant oases in which magnificent forests concealed an abundance of wildlife, both feathered and furred, and grape vines and edible plants grew in profusion. Nor did he take into consideration that the friendly Indians at Croatoan (today's Hatteras Island) were, like others of the native Americans, experts at survival under drought conditions, especially when surrounded by waters teeming with fish and oysters. While it is quite possible that members of the colony died of diseases brought on by malnutrition, later evidence indicates that a few of them, at least, lived on for many years.

This brings us to the conclusion reached by Hamilton McMillan, and widely supported by subsequent investigators, that the Croatan Indians, residing primarily in Robeson County, are the direct descendants of Ananias and Eleanor Dare and their fellow lost colonists. In essence, McMillan's conclusion was that the Hatteras Indians, described by John Lawson in the early 1700s as claiming descent from white people who "could talk in a Book as we do," had migrated over two hundred miles westward to the Lumber River area, where McMillan found them nearly two centuries later.

McMillan based his claim on a combination of factors, with emphasis on the family names, remnant "Anglo-Saxon" speech, and Indian traditions; however, the contention by McMillan and Stephen B. Weeks that an amazingly large percentage of the names of the colonists were still to be found among the "Croatans" has since been seriously challenged. There were, for example, no Croatans named Dare, the names cited by McMillan being "Darr,

Durr, and Dorr," and most of the other colonists' surnames were and are fairly common. What was represented
as the remnant of early "Anglo-Saxon" speech is, in reality, a dialect not dissimilar to others found in the eastern
United States, especially in isolated areas. The official
designation of the Robeson County tribe as Croatan Indians was meaningless, since it was done under pressure
from McMillan and the Indians themselves.

Most of the other evidence used to support the Lumbee
theory is shaky at best, and among the shakiest bits is the
claim of the Reverend Morgan Jones that he found Welsh-
speaking Indians, the Doegs, living near the Pamlico River
in 1660. Only five of the lost colonists had bona fide
Welsh surnames (three Joneses and two Powells), and
similar claims were later made—and disproven—about
the Delaware, Shawnee, Comanche, and over a dozen
other tribes. Equally suspect is John Lederer's report of a
"powerful Nation of Bearded men," for he only heard of
them while he was tarrying near a large, brackish lake,
later proven to be nonexistent, in the Carolina Piedmont. The beardless Indian myth is further weakened by
Thomas Hariot's observation that the men of Pomeiooc
were growing beards before the lost colonists arrived.

One telling piece of evidence remains to be dealt with.
Lawson cited the tradition that the Hatteras Indians were
descended from Raleigh's colonists, and an elderly member of the Lumbees of Robeson County had always heard
that his ancestors came from "Roanoke in Virginia." The
first to point out a reasonable alternative explanation for
the apparent connection between the lost colonists and
the Lumbees was Samuel A'Court Ashe, who said that it
was entirely possible for some of the Robeson County
Indians to be descended from Raleigh's settlers, but *not*
from the lost colonists. "There were," he said, "other op-
portunities for an admixture of the races. Thirty-two men
of Captain Raymond's company were among them [the
Croatan Indians] twenty days before the arrival of Lane's

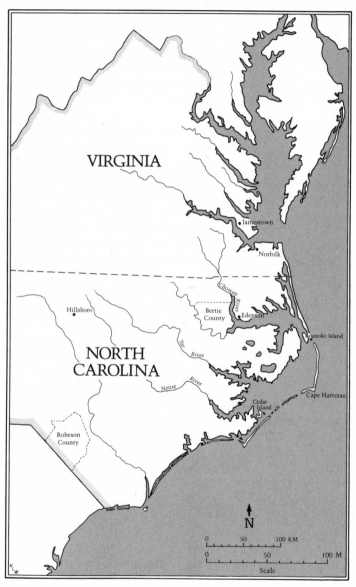

MAP 6. *Searching for the lost colony.*

colony, and the following summer Captain Stafford and twenty men were with them until Drake came in June, and doubtless others were stationed there the next year to keep watch for the expected return of White." This is not to rule out entirely the possibility that descendants of the lost colonists themselves are still to be found in Robeson County, but certainly there is no direct proof.

If these theories are to be discounted or minimized in the process of winnowing out clues and claims, what then remains as valid evidence worthy of further consideration? For those who have followed the matter closely, the answer is obvious: The Jamestown settlers were the only people who actually tried to make contact with any living lost colonists, and they came close on several occasions. In many instances their firsthand reports were recorded by several different principals in the expedition, giving us two or more accounts of the same occurrence.

As they explored the territory to the west of Jamestown, always seeking and usually securing information from the local weroances, they heard over and over again of men clothed like the settlers, some at Ocanahonan and Peccarecanick and still others farther inland, at Ritanoe and Panawicke. Then the story of Powhatan's actions began to emerge. His priests—Quiyoughquisocks or Quiyoughquohanocks—had persuaded him that "the men, women and children of the first plantation at Roanoak . . . who 20. and od yeares had peaceably lyved and intermixed with those Savadges, and were out of his Territory," were nonetheless a threat to his confederacy, and shortly before the arrival of the Jamestown settlers Powhatan had launched an attack against them.

According to the Indians many of the lost colonists were slaughtered, but some survived. At least seven—"fower men, twoo Boyes, and one young Maid"—were at Ritanoe, working with the cooper extracted from the mines of the weroance Eyanoco. Others were reported to be even closer to Jamestown—"within fifty mile of our fort"—apparently in the Chowan River area. John Smith sent out at least two parties to find the lost colonists, the first led by Michael Sicklemore and the second including Nathaniell Powell and Anas Todkill. But Powhatan, who later confessed "that he had been at the murder of that colony," sent his "bloudy and furious" priests as guides, and the search efforts ended in frustration. The final report stated simply: "Nothing could we learne but they were all dead."

In 1959 three distinguished scholars met on the stage of the Waterside Theatre at Fort Raleigh during intermission of *The Lost Colony* to exchange their views on what had happened to the Roanoke colonists. They were the late C. Christopher Crittenden, director of the North Carolina Department of Archives and History, who had studied and written about the mystery for many years; William S. Powell, now professor of history at the University of North Carolina, who had only recently returned from a sabbatical in England, where he had studied the life histories of individual colonists; and David Beers Quinn, universally recognized, then and now, as the authority on the subject by virtue of his extensive research and his authorship of the definitive, two-volume *Roanoke Voyages*.

Here are the conclusions of the panel, agreed to by all three members:

1. The Spaniards did not attack the colonists.
2. The Eleanor Dare stones and the Eleanor Dare diary were fakes.
3. The colonists did not have a vessel large enough to carry all of them, and if some attempted to sail home to England, others had to be left behind.
4. The colonists intended to leave Roanoke Island and move to Croatan, and some, at least, did just that.
5. At the time they left Roanoke Island, or later from Croatan, some of them undoubtedly moved to the

interior, probably splitting up into two or more groups.

6. Though it is possible that some of them ended up in what is now Robeson County, it is more probable that their destination was the Chowan River area or the south side of Chesapeake Bay, with which they were already familiar.

7. Almost certainly, Powhatan slaughtered some of the colonists. But it was general practice among the Indians to spare the women and children in such attacks, and apparently some men escaped as well.

8. Finally, a number of the colonists undoubtedly remained alive for many years after being abandoned on Roanoke Island, and some of them, at least, were still alive and living with friendly Indians shortly before the arrival of the Jamestown colony.

In the period of nearly a quarter of a century since this panel was convened no substantive additional material has been uncovered—though speculation about the fate of the colonists has intensified.

Quinn seems convinced now that most of the colonists, including "all family groups, children and most of the single men," joined the Chesapeake Indians in the area now occupied by the cities of Virginia Beach and Chesapeake. He admits, however, that such a conclusion as to their exact destination and the composition of the surviving party is based more on conjecture than on evidence.

Additional credence must now be given to the possibility advanced by Lefler and Newsome that the main body of the colonists, "finally despairing of relief, sailed for England in a boat which had been left with them by White in 1587, and were lost in the Atlantic." Regardless of their destination when leaving the protection of their fort, the fact is that Roanoke is an island, and the colonists could have traveled only by boat. There is the additional possibility, therefore, that some or most of them could have perished in a shipwreck on that highly exposed part of the North Carolina coast.

Extensive archaeological work is now being undertaken in connection with the four hundredth anniversary of the Roanoke Island settlements. But even if these efforts result in the discovery of artifacts of European origin in the Indian village sites along the Chowan River, Albemarle Sound, or the lower reaches of the Chesapeake, the result might be that the mystery is deepened rather than solved. For it must be remembered that the 116 men, women, and children left by White in 1587 were not the only Europeans to visit the area prior to the arrival of the permanent settlers at Jamestown. There were two other Raleigh "lost colonies"—the 3 men abandoned by Lane when he returned to England with Drake; and the 15 men left on Roanoke Island by Grenville.

There are strong indications also that Spanish friars had already attempted to establish an outpost on Chesapeake Bay before the English arrived, leaving the possibility that survivors intermingled with the natives. And not to be overlooked are the Indian tales of other white men shipwrecked on the coast some twenty years prior to the Amadas and Barlowe expedition, as well as tantalizing hints that still others, including slaves captured by Drake in the Caribbean, might have ended up on the North American mainland.

What happened to the lost colony? No one really knows —and very likely no one ever will. The fate of Raleigh's colonists remains as much a mystery as before.

Conclusion

The search for the lost colony goes forward. No doubt it will continue so long as inquisitive men and women dig holes in the ground in the search for artifacts, or seek out long-hidden records of times past. But whether or not their research turns up additional information on the fate of Virginia Dare and her fellow settlers, this much is certain: the record of Sir Walter Raleigh's colonization efforts makes clear that the history of English-speaking America began four hundred years ago, not at Jamestown or Plymouth Rock as so many are led to believe, but at Roanoke Island.

Raleigh's people founded there the first English settlement in America. More than 100 Englishmen, under Ralph Lane, lived for a year on Roanoke Island, using it as a base for extensive exploration of the river and sound country in northeastern North Carolina and the fringes of Chesapeake Bay in Virginia. During the period from the spring of 1584 until late summer of 1587 some fifty English vessels called at Hatorask and the other ports of entry along the Outer Banks, and more than 1,000 Englishmen viewed or visited those low-lying barrier islands.

Widespread speculation on the fate of the lost colonists has overshadowed the more important question of why the effort failed. How close they came! How often decisions of seemingly little importance at the time changed the course of history! Why did Grenville leave only 107 men on Roanoke Island to establish the first colony under Lane in 1585, when he had several times that many available aboard his ships? How could Lane have failed to anticipate the consequences of his decision to attack Dasamonquepeuc, under pretense of friendship, and murder the weroance Wingina? Why didn't he leave a small garrison at the fort when he returned to England with Drake? Why didn't the captain of Raleigh's relief ship remain in the area for the anticipated arrival of Grenville's main force in 1586? And above all, why did Grenville decide to leave only 15 men on Roanoke Island to hold a continent?

One can speculate on the motives behind Ferdinando's decision not to transport White's colonists to Chesapeake Bay in 1587; on whether White would have found his colonists alive had he reached Roanoke Island on the ill-fated 1588 voyage; on why no effort was made to send out a relief expedition in 1589; and, finally, on whether there would have been a lost colony mystery at all if White and the 1590 relief expedition had not dawdled so long in the Caribbean, or if, after reaching the Outer Banks, they had gone directly to Roanoke Island instead of wasting a day tramping down the beach toward distant smoke from a brush fire.

That the Roanoke Island experiment was disorganized, even by sixteenth-century standards, is quite apparent; yet it led two decades later to permanent settlement on the Chesapeake. In a broader sense, this establishment of a North American outpost by England was a forerunner of a vast network of colonies that came in time to encompass the globe.

Rumors and folk tales, on which history is so often based, serve to titillate the imagination; but written records, and especially those with pictorial illumination, stamp events indelibly on the minds of men. The published accounts of Barlowe, Lane, and Grenville, and especially of Hariot—and the drawings and personal narratives of John White—created in the English public in the late sixteenth century an interest in overseas colonization that did not diminish with the passage of time. The documents relating to the Roanoke Island colonies have provided historians with unique information, not only about the little-understood Indians of North Carolina and Virginia, but about life in Elizabethan England as well.

The conviction shared by leaders of the Jamestown settlement that remnants of the lost colony had borne up for more than twenty years under the worst the Indians and the environment could dish out undoubtedly gave them hope during their bleakest moments. And the fact that some of the leading backers of the Jamestown effort were individuals closely associated with the Roanoke Island settlement provided a sense of continuity so often lacking when foreigners attempt to take possession of alien territory.

No matter that the initial effort failed, or that the last Roanoke Island colonists became lost colonists. The very fact that Raleigh's people established their claim in the name of Elizabeth, built a fort and houses, and opened a discourse with the natives, gave notice that England intended to stay Spain's northward occupation of the American mainland. Had it been otherwise, those of us living here today might well be speaking Spanish instead of English.

A Note on Sources

Basic information on the Raleigh colonization efforts is found in books printed in the late sixteenth century and thus not accessible to the average reader. For the individual interested in further study on the subject, however, reasonably priced reprints are now available.

Thomas Hariot's *A Briefe and True Report of the New Found Land of Virginia*, published by Theodor de Bry in 1590, was reprinted in facsimile in 1972 by Dover Publications. Included are a number of de Bry's engravings of the John White drawings, as well as an informative introduction by Paul Hulton of the British Museum.

The accounts of the various participants in the Roanoke Island venture appeared in the two-volume English edition of Richard Hakluyt's *The Principall Navigations . . . of the English Nation* in 1589. All of these accounts, plus considerable additional material, have been brought together by David B. Quinn and Alison M. Quinn in *The First Colonists: Documents on the Planting of the First English Settlements in North America, 1584–1590*, issued by the North Carolina Department of Cultural Resources in 1982 as the first in a series of books sponsored by America's Four Hundredth Anniversary Committee.

The third basic source of information, John White's watercolor paintings, was published by the British Museum and the University of North Carolina Press in 1964 under the title *The American Drawings of John White,* edited by Paul Hulton and David B. Quinn. Only six hundred copies were printed, and the edition has long been out of print. A popularly priced reprint is scheduled for publication in 1984 under the same joint auspices, and with sponsorship by America's Four Hundredth Anniversary Committee.

More serious students of the subject will find a number of other pertinent documents and a wealth of additional background information in David B. Quinn's *The Roanoke Voyages*, published in two volumes by the Hakluyt Society, London, in 1955.

More than fifty other printed works were consulted as this book took shape. Where appropriate, they have been identified in the text.

Glossary

admiral: 1. A high-ranking naval officer, above a captain, often in charge of a fleet. 2. In Elizabethan times, a person in command of two or more naval or civilian ships. 3. An admiral's ship (see *flagship*).

Algonkians: A large group of Indian tribes, related mostly by language, that includes the Cree, Cheyenne, Delaware, and many others, living and extinct. Most of the tribes living in northeastern North Carolina in the 1580s probably spoke Algonkian languages, although they were not politically united.

bark: A general term for square-rigged ships of thirty to over two hundred tons.

bastion: A projecting part of a fortification.

breach: A shoal or other feature on which waves break.

capstan: A vertical drum used on a ship to raise anchors, hoist heavy sails, and take in lines. The manual capstan of the sixteenth century was turned by pushing against wooden bars inserted into "pigeon holes" in the top of the drum.

captain: 1. The commander of a ship (see also *master*). 2. An army officer in charge of a company or troop.

Chawanoacs: An Algonkian tribe living west of the Chowan River in 1585–86.

Chesepians: An Algonkian tribe living at the south

end of Chesapeake Bay in the sixteenth and seventeenth centuries.

consort: 1. A ship that accompanies another. 2. A group of musicians.

corsair: A pirate (originally a Barbary pirate) or privateer (see *privateer*).

Croatans: See *Lumbees*.

Croatoans: Manteo's tribe, apparently Algonkian, which lived on the island of Croatoan, near modern Cape Hatteras. See also *Hatteras Indians*.

Doegs: Welsh-speaking Indians whom the Reverend Morgan Jones claimed to have found living in Tuscarora country near the Pamlico River. The name may be related to *Mandoags* (see *Mangoaks*).

fjord: A long, deep, narrow arm of the sea between cliffs or steep slopes.

flagship: A ship on which an admiral or other officer in command of a group of ships normally rides.

flyboat: Any of several types of fast sailing ship, usually of forty to one hundred and fifty tons. Originally, a *flyboat* was a small Dutch sailing craft used on the Vlie, the passage between the Zuider Zee and the North Sea.

Guiana: The sixteenth-century name for northeastern South America, especially the part between the Orinoco and Amazon rivers.

Gulf Stream: The popular name for the warm oceanic currents that flow from the Straits of Florida to Cape Hatteras (the Florida Current), from Cape Hatteras to the Grand Banks of Newfoundland (the Gulf Stream proper), and from the Grand Banks to northwestern Europe (the North Atlantic Drift).

Haliwar Indians: A triracial group living in Halifax and Warren counties, North Carolina, supposed by some to include descendants of the lost colonists.

Hatteras Indians: Indians living near Cape Hatteras in the eighteenth century—probably descendants of

the Croatoans of the 1580s. By the end of the eighteenth century the tribe had died out or joined the
Mattamuskeets on the mainland.

impress: 1. To take private goods for public use. 2. To
compel men to serve in the navy or army.

jarl: A Norse chief or nobleman. The word is related
to the English *earl*.

Kewas: An idol of the type worshiped by the Roanoacs and neighboring Algonkian tribes. The plural
is *Kewasowak*.

lighter: A small craft used to load and unload larger
vessels.

littoral drift: Weak inshore oceanic currents created
by waves striking the shore obliquely. Along the
east coast of the United States, littoral drift is generally southward.

longbow: A bow, usually five to six feet long, developed in the late Middle Ages. Because it had greater
range than most shoulder guns and could be fired
faster than a crossbow, it was still a useful weapon
in the sixteenth century.

Lumbees (also Croatans, Pembrokes, and Redbones):
A large triracial group living around the Lumber
River in North Carolina and South Carolina, believed by some to contain descendants of the lost
colony.

maize: Indian corn.

Malungeons: A small triracial group living in and
around Hancock County, Tennessee, alleged to include descendants of the lost colony. The name
may come from the French *mélange*, "mixture."

Mangoaks (also Mandoags): A tribe, possibly
Iroquoian, living along the upper Roanoke River in
1586. The name, which may be Carolina Algonkian
for "rattlesnakes," could have signified the Tuscarora.

master: 1. The captain of a civilian ship. 2. The officer responsible for navigation and steering on a naval vessel, not necessarily the captain.

Moratucks: A tribe living south of the lower Morotico (Roanoke) River in 1586.

Neiosiokes: A tribe of unknown linguistic affiliation living along the lower Neuse River in the 1580s.

northeaster: A gale or strong wind from the northeast.

Norumbega: The sixteenth-century name for New England and the Maritime Provinces of Canada.

patent: An official license to exercise a privilege, such as exploring, privateering, or establishing a monopoly.

periwig: A wig, especially of the type worn by European men in the sixteenth, seventeenth, and eighteenth centuries. Periwigs came in several styles but were usually long in the back and curly on the sides.

pike: A metal-tipped wooden spear, normally ten to twenty feet long.

pinnace: Any of several types of relatively small vessels, often used as tenders or consorts. Pinnaces could have one, two, or three masts and range from ten to fifty tons; some, such as the one built in Puerto Rico by Grenville's men, could be rowed as well as sailed; some were undecked.

Powhatan: The leader of the Powhatan Confederation in the early seventeenth century. It is not clear whether the term is a personal name or a title.

Powhatan Confederation: A large group of Algonkian tribes living along the western shore of Chesapeake Bay in the seventeenth century. Surviving tribes include the triracial Pamunkey and Chickahominy.

privateer: A private citizen authorized by one country to attack another country's ships, distinct from a pirate, who attacks ships without anyone's permission.

Roanoacs: The Algonkian tribe living on Roanoke Island and the nearby mainland in the 1580s.

saker shot: Iron shot used in a *saker*, a type of small-bore cannon often mounted on ships.

shoal: An underwater sand bar or sand bank.

slough: An underwater depression.

sound: A long, fairly wide estuary or arm of the sea.

tender: A small craft used to maintain and carry cargo, passengers, and messages to and from a larger vessel.

tilt boat: A large rowboat fitted with an awning.

triracial group: A mixture of three races—in the examples above, American Indians, Negroes, and whites.

Vinland: The area of North America settled by Leif Eriksson in the eleventh century, which authorities have placed in various locations from North Carolina to Labrador.

Weapemeocs: An Algonkian tribe living north of Albemarle Sound in the late 1580s.

weir: A fencelike or mazelike structure used to confuse and trap fish.

weroance: A term used by Raleigh's colonists to denote, at various times, an Indian king, chief, or nobleman.

wherry: A long, double-ended rowboat, usually carrying two oars per side. The larger double wherry had four oars per side.

Index